THE AMERICAN REVOLUTION
CONSIDERED AS A SOCIAL MOVEMENT

THE AMERICAN REVOLUTION CONSIDERED AS A SOCIAL MOVEMENT

100TH ANNIVERSARY EDITION

J. Franklin Jameson

With a new foreword by
Michael A. Blaakman and
Sarah Barringer Gordon

PRINCETON UNIVERSITY PRESS

PRINCETON & OXFORD

Published by Princeton University Press
41 William Street, Princeton, New Jersey 08540
99 Banbury Road, Oxford OX2 6JX

press.princeton.edu

GPSR Authorized Representative: Easy Access System Europe - Mustamäe tee 50, 10621 Tallinn, Estonia, gpsr.requests@easproject.com

ISBN 9780691280813
ISBN (paperback) 9780691275031
ISBN (ebook) 9780691275048

Library of Congress Control Number: 2025940536

Lectures delivered in November 1925 on the Louis Clark Vanuxem Foundation

British Library Cataloging-in-Publication Data is available

Editorial: Dave McBride and Alena Chekanov
Production Editorial: Terri O'Prey
Jacket/Cover Design: Heather Hansen
Production: Erin Suydam
Publicity: Natalie Zander

Cover image: Sprengel, M. C, Daniel Chodowiecki, D Berger. *Allgemeines historisches Taschenbuch oder Abriss der merkwürdigsten neuen Welt-Begebenheiten enthaltend für 1784 die Geschichte der Revolution von Nord-America.* Berlin: Bey Haude und Spener, 1784. Courtesy of the Anne S.K. Brown Military Collection / John Hay Library / Brown University Library.

This book has been composed in Miller

10 9 8 7 6 5 4 3 2 1

CONTENTS

In November 1925, J. Franklin Jameson, Chief of the Manuscripts Division and Benjamin Chair in American History at the Library of Congress, delivered four lectures at Princeton University that were subsequently published as *The American Revolution Considered as a Social Movement.* The book is now a century old, and its topic, the American Revolution, is 250. Jameson had been working on his theories of the Revolution for thirty years before they were published. In other words, these lectures on history have a rich history of their own. Like the Revolution itself, they had been underway for decades before they took their final form.[1]

Jameson's lectures explored what he called the "the stream of revolution," which "could not be confined within narrow banks, but spread abroad upon the land." In Jameson's hands, the effects of the Revolution, rather than its cause or its battles, took center stage, an innovative approach that shifted attention away from high politics and the strategies of generals to ordinary life and the changes that accompanied and followed the long revolutionary conflict.[2]

1. J. Franklin Jameson to Charles Beard, August 10, 1926, in *An Historian's World: Selections from the Correspondence of John Franklin Jameson,* ed. Elizabeth Donnan and Leo F. Stock (American Philosophical Society, 1956), 319.

2. J. Franklin Jameson, *The American Revolution Considered as a Social Movement* (Princeton University Press, 2025 [orig. 1926]), 7. Unless otherwise noted, all citations of Jameson's book refer to the present edition.

Jameson divided these "social consequences" of the Revolution into four broad topics. The first is the "status of persons," which included white male suffrage, racial slavery, and the growth of antislavery sentiment in the immediate aftermath of the Revolution. Second is "the land," especially the confiscation of loyalist real and personal property, and the breaking up of enormous estates that had been granted by the British king to his imperial officials. The broader effects of "freeing the soil" to be transformed into modest farms, Jameson argued, were crucial to democracy. Third, "industry and commerce" had not been abandoned during the years of the war, but enterprising merchants, farmers, and manufacturers were freed after 1783 and the Treaty of Paris from the "fetters" of imperial monopolies on commerce. Now, their products flowed into "new channels of trade." Finally, the fourth chapter, awkwardly titled "thought and feeling," concludes that "religious freedom and equality [are] America's chief contribution to the world's civilization" and touches as well on nationalism, public opinion, and education. Jameson ended with the central importance of social history, calling for attention to "all the varied activities of men in the same country and period," because society cannot be cleaved off into a category separate from other dimensions of the past.[3]

Jameson delivered his lectures to the brand-new history department at Princeton. If what we know about his style as a teacher is a guide to how he delivered these lectures, he spoke formally and without emotion. Jameson was not a

3. Jameson, *American Revolution Considered as a Social Movement*, 9, 49, 69, 90, 100.

crowd pleaser. His most loyal acolytes argued that advanced and sophisticated minds, especially those already in graduate school, appreciated Jameson, while the less cultivated missed the point (one can imagine what the freshmen thought).[4]

The following year, Princeton University Press published the lectures as a short book. Concise, evocative, and "serenely engaging," the four chapters retain the aura of their first instantiation as lectures. There are no footnotes and precious little reference to related scholarship—both essential elements of what Jameson and others called "scientific history." Perhaps because they do not engage directly with the historiography of the Revolution (which Jameson argued was narrow and unimaginative), the lectures are surprisingly readable.[5]

The lectures and the book that followed were timed carefully, of course, to mark the 150th anniversary of the American Revolution. Jameson began by observing that important anniversaries in American history had already

4. Jameson acknowledged in 1903 that he was not "a first-rate teacher." Jameson to Francis A. Christie, March 6, 1903, in Donnan and Stock, *Historian's World*, 85–86. Waldo Gifford Leland, "Jameson, John Franklin," *Dictionary of American Biography*, suppl. 2 (Scribner, 1958), 339–44, wrote that Jameson's teaching career at Brown was hampered by "his austere appearance and exacting standards of scholastic performance" (340). "As a teacher Jameson was at his best with graduate students, many of whom achieved high reputations as scholars and all of whom held him in warm affection and admiration" (344). (Leland was among the many protégés whose careers were affected—and likely aided—by Jameson's patronage.)

5. Charles A. Beard, "A Challenge to Windbags," *New Republic*, August 11, 1926, 344. On scientific history and Jameson's role in insisting on that "modern" approach to historical research and writing, see Peter Novick, *That Noble Dream: The "Objectivity Question" and the American Historical Profession* (Cambridge University Press, 1988), 32–39, 42–46, 51–57.

proven productive for American historians. The centennial of the Declaration of Independence in 1876, Jameson noted, caught the attention of the public in ways that enlivened historical research and expanded the scope of historical writing. The centennial also drew students to the focused study of the American past and prompted colleges and universities to establish new professorships in history. Anniversaries were good for business.

It was telling that Jameson began his lectures by celebrating the growth of history as a professional field. His long career was dedicated primarily to promoting the development of the field as a whole, building structures, resources, and institutions that could support others as they produced great work. In that sense, he was not a conventional scholarly practitioner. Jameson described himself not as a successful historian of the kind he admired most: someone whose work wrestled deep archival research to the ground and analyzed it in a major monograph of door-stopping proportions. Rather, he once mused, his main contribution to the emerging discipline of history lay in the heuristic quality of his writings and his mentorship.[6]

With these lectures, though, Jameson put his hand on the scale. The fruit of decades dedicated to collecting and editing archival documents, promoting careful research, and reading and contemplating fine scholarship, Jameson's four lectures argued that the American Revolution was far more interesting than historians had recognized. His was the first

6. Jameson to Woodrow Wilson, May 12, 1922, in Donnan and Stock, *Historian's World*, 270.

and most important argument that studying the Revolution should involve broad social, economic, literary, religious, racial, and legal matters. He also explored how the Revolution failed to produce some results that one would have hoped it could deliver, such as the end of slavery. When understood from Jameson's critical and broad-ranging perspective, the Revolution appeared more varied and wide-ranging, bigger than battles and political oratory. The Revolution was not the sole purview of antiquarians and reverent nationalists, he argued. Rather, it was an exciting topic begging for new research and reinterpretation by experts.

A century after this book's first publication, and at the 250th anniversary of the Declaration of Independence, the historical discipline once again faces immense challenges. In such a moment, Jameson's efforts to build institutional support for historical research and scholarship seem more significant—and more relevant—than ever. In the following pages, we therefore revisit Jameson's deep commitment to the development of the profession, as well as the influence of his argument in this volume. With this 100th-anniversary edition, we invite the reader to reconsider the Revolution and to draw inspiration from Jameson's insistence that it can (and should) be seen anew.

⟨━━━━◗▓◖━━━━⟩

Generations of graduate students have read *The American Revolution Considered as a Social Movement.* Despite their enduring resonance with scholars of the Revolution, the lectures and the resulting volume were not universally admired in his day, even by those who greatly valued Jameson. At his death in late 1937, the *American Historical Review* published a memorial essay based on "information and comment generously given by a number of Dr. Jameson's former students and associates." This book was not mentioned. Critics are still vocal.[7]

During his lifetime, Jameson was better known for work that has since been overlooked, even forgotten. His field-building efforts (many but not all successful) were crucially important to the study of history in the United States. His influence and often his generosity were critical to the growth of the field. Jameson recognized that fine historical research and writing required substantial investment in collecting and organizing records of all kinds. He also understood that the other half of the coin was supportive institutions and organizations that would recognize and promote scholarly work. Soon after Jameson was awarded the first American PhD degree in history by Johns Hopkins University in 1882, he began what would become a lifelong undertaking: he founded, led, funded, and served organizations designed to support and sustain professional history and those who worked in the field. At the same time, he undertook an extraordinary and sustained program to collect and publish documents and manuscripts relevant to historical topics. In other words, he diagnosed the weaknesses of the field, and then he set out to remedy them.[8]

7. "John Franklin Jameson," *American Historical Review* 43, no. 2 (1938): 243–52.

8. Morey D. Rothberg, "The Brahmin as Bureaucrat: J. Franklin Jameson at the Carnegie Institution of Washington, 1905–1928," *The Public Historian* 8, no. 4 (1986): 49; Arthur Schlesinger Sr., introduction to *The American*

Jameson's own education was marred by fits and starts, and especially by his relative poverty—in ways that redounded to the benefit of American historical scholarship. His family's lack of financial resources kept him close to home. Initially, his father had been a schoolmaster, but when his school closed in the late 1870s, he moved to Amherst, started a solo legal practice, and became postmaster. The young Jameson, who already had been admitted to Harvard, reluctantly shifted to Amherst College, doubtless because his family could not afford his living expenses in Cambridge.[9] He was a star student at Amherst, and there he found his vocation: American history, both as a topic of study and as a professional field. Jameson hoped to study abroad like other aspiring historians, who trained mostly at German universities. But his family could not afford the several thousand dollars it would take to travel to and live in Germany. Instead, Jameson struggled miserably with a one-year job teaching high school in Worcester, Massachusetts. The students ran roughshod over the greenhorn teacher, and he promptly shifted gears. He entered graduate school in history at Johns Hopkins, where he studied with Herbert Baxter Adams, another Amherst alumnus. Jameson focused on institution-building in the colonial and early Republic eras, with a dissertation titled "The Origin and Development of the Municipal Government of New York City." He received

---

Revolution Considered as a Social Movement, by J. Franklin Jameson (Beacon Press, 1956), vii.

9. As his biographer noted, Jameson "lived at home all four years." Morey D. Rothberg, "Jameson, John Franklin," *American National Biography*, 1, https://doi.org/10.1093/anb/9780198606697.article.1400317.

his degree in 1882 and stayed on for six additional years as a fellow and instructor.[10]

Jameson not only came to understand what might be useful to those trained in the field as he found it in the 1880s, he also looked ahead toward those who would come later. He was dismayed, for example, that of the few academics whose work was mostly in history, almost none focused on American topics, his own primary interest. The documents to sustain such work, he soon recognized, simply were not available, especially for the colonial and early national periods. With characteristic *savoir faire*, he began to devise a plan: he would send scholars to archives abroad, mostly in Britain and Europe, to collect copies of documents relevant to American history. Over the next fifty years, Jameson assembled and published massive collections of primary documents that would sustain research going forward.

He was an entrepreneurial historian who constantly thought ahead and worked to create and nurture the architecture of the discipline of history and the careers of historians. In the 1880s, even without a professorship of his own, Jameson began to exhibit a remarkable ability to advance the profession (and sometimes his own career) by becoming a keen observer of his fellow historians. As one of the earliest home-grown historians in the country, Jameson was in on the ground floor of the field. He was present at the founding of the American Historical Association in 1884 at Saratoga

10. The dissertation eventually was published as two articles. On this lackluster beginning of Jameson's career, see Alfred F. Young and Gregory H. Nobles, *Whose American Revolution Was It? Historians Interpret the Founding* (New York University Press, 2011), 27–28.

Springs. Apparently, Jameson was not impressed, especially as a young historian who needed a permanent job. At this inaugural meeting, he said, there was a dearth of "men from whom a job may sometime come."[11] Despite this inauspicious beginning, Jameson came to value the Association deeply and used it as a springboard for the formation of other key institutions that have become central to the field of history.

Jameson's love of history did not translate into talented teaching, even though his mentorship became important to two generations of historians. In 1889, he finally was hired by Brown University in Rhode Island, which one biographer dismissed as a "small Baptist school" in the late nineteenth century. He taught there until 1901. His Brown colleague and future university president E. Benjamin Andrews—whose brilliant and popular teaching as professor of history and political economy made Jameson's classroom performance pale by comparison—was criticized for his political views by the school's trustees. Jameson led a successful counterattack among faculty when Andrews resigned. Jameson's "Open Letter" addressed to the "Corporation of Brown University by the Members of the Faculty" in 1897 has become a classic defense of academic freedom, yet another contribution from Jameson to the professional architecture of his field.[12]

11. Diary, September 10, 1884, J. Franklin Jameson Papers, Manuscript Division, Library of Congress (quoted in Rothberg, "Brahmin as Bureaucrat," 54).

12. Elizabeth Donnan, "A Nineteenth-Century Academic Cause Célèbre," *New England Quarterly* 25, no. 1 (1952): 23–46; Waldo Gifford Leland, "Jameson, John Franklin," *Dictionary of American Biography*, suppl. 2 (C. Scribner's Sons, 1958), 341.

By then, Jameson was already looking to leave Brown. He had hoped to land a job at Barnard in New York City, and in 1895 he delivered there the first version of what became his Princeton lectures three decades later. The job offer followed, but Jameson considered the salary paltry and turned it down. Finally, he was recruited as head of the history department at the University of Chicago, where he taught from 1901 to 1905. Yet again Jameson did not flourish. He complained bitterly about the perceived social (and actual physical) coldness of Chicago and its environs.[13]

During his tenure in Chicago, Jameson learned that his Hopkins advisor Herbert Baxter Adams left $5,000 to the American Historical Association at his death in 1901.[14] Jameson determined to use the funds to respond to a provocative lecture by the young historian Lucy Salmon of Vassar College, who had called for the establishment of a "School of Historical Studies," like the American academies in Berlin and Rome, where graduate students and early career scholars might stay while doing their research and receive the advice of distinguished scholars in the area.[15]

13. Jameson to Francis A. Christie, March 6, 1903, in Donnan and Stock, *Historian's World*, 85.

14. John Martin Vincent, "Herbert B. Adams: A Memorial Address," *Annual Report of the American Historical Association for the Year 1901* (Government Printing Office, 1902), 1:199–210.

15. "Lucy Maynard Salmon," *Encyclopedia Britannica*, https://www.britannica.com/biography/Lucy-Maynard-Salmon; Mary R. Dearing, "Hope for the Young Scholar: An Unrealized Dream," in *J. Franklin Jameson: A Tribute*, ed. Ruth Anna Fisher and William Lloyd Fox (Catholic University of America Press, 1965), 47–49.

The AHA executive council appointed Jameson and two others to evaluate the idea. In late 1901, just as the committee began its work, Andrew Carnegie announced a $10 million gift to create the Carnegie Institute in Washington to support "investigation in any department of science, literature or art." Jameson wrote to the president of the new institute, arguing that a school of historical research could train graduate students, as well as catalogue manuscripts and other significant historical documents, establish a dictionary of national biography, commission a historical atlas, subsidize publication of the *American Historical Review*, and more.[16]

This was Jameson's longstanding wish list. Within months, the Carnegie Institute invited the members of the AHA committee, led by Jameson, to review his own proposals and report back to the executive committee. Despite some disagreement among the three members, their report and recommendations were adopted by the institute in early 1903. Yet, in 1903 the trustees appointed committee member Andrew McLaughlin, rather than Jameson, to run the new Bureau of Historical Research and edit the *American Historical Review*. McLaughlin was surprised but took the job, even while noting that Jameson would be "the best man" for it. Just two years later, McLaughlin was recruited from the post by the University of Chicago. Jameson was delighted to trade places.[17]

16. "Articles of Incorporation," January 4, 1902, reprinted in *The Carnegie Institution of Washington, D.C.* (Washington, DC, 1902), 5; Jameson to Daniel Coit Gilman, February 14, 1902, in Donnan and Stock, *Historian's World*, 79–82.

17. "Andrew C. McLaughlin: In Memoriam," *American Historical Review* 53, no. 2 (1948): 432–34.

Jameson's move to Washington in late 1905 allowed him for the first time to work in the place where American history was made (and would be recorded, if Jameson had his way). Finally, he was able to leave teaching and dive into what he wanted to do most. He also valued deeply the opportunity to be at the center of politics and policy. In the nation's capital, Jameson was in the eye of the storm. Like others of his era, he believed that a modern understanding of history that focused on ordinary lives would be critically important in fashioning a new approach to government. This approach would rely on "expertise," including historical training. Experts and their work would then take their due place at the helm of the ship of state, deploying scientific methods to understand society and craft cautious policy. For Jameson, this required a concerted turn to historical records. Recovery of the truths of history, in other words, would bring wisdom into the halls of government. Supporting efficient administration and popular will, while at the same time arguing against placing power in the hands of "a vast horde of unintelligent farmers [and] demagogues," Jameson aimed to balance democracy with centralized government. His long friendship with Woodrow Wilson, who shared Jameson's belief in the necessity of institutional bases for good government, linked politics and historicism. In Washington, both men found fellow travelers and scope for their historical liberalism, tempered with the goal of administrative efficiency and efficacy. For Jameson, the past became a resource for discerning "what will succeed."[18]

18. J. Franklin Jameson, "The Future Uses of History," *History Teacher's Magazine* 4 (February 1913): 37–38; Morey D. Rothberg, "Servant to History: A Study of John Franklin Jameson" (PhD diss., Brown University, 1983),

Washington also became the home of the American Historical Association. As purveyors of a new way of learning and knowing, Jameson and other historians of his generation trained their institution-building ambitions on the place where the future was decided. The Association was formally chartered by Congress in 1889, for the promotion of historical studies and research, evidence that Congress also understood the significance of the new science of history. Assembling and organizing the records that memorialized decision-making was also an essential goal. By recovering past records and ensuring that present decisions were duly recorded, historians would fulfill their obligation to study the past and preserve the present for future generations. Jameson saw himself as the driver of the train; his diligence and considerable talent were suited to the atmosphere of the capital, where he stayed until his death in 1937.[19]

Jameson directed the Department of Historical Research at the Carnegie Institute for more than two decades. In that period, funding for publication of multiple volumes of documents collected at home and abroad meant that new vistas opened for historical knowledge and research. The documentary projects Jameson oversaw included colonial and Revolutionary-era collections of British imperial records, assembled documents on pirates and privateers (focused

---

125–26. Jameson trusted scientific history to find the "truth." As the historian Dorothy Ross put it, Jameson "could find in history a useable past and leave the difficulties of its uses to others." Ross, *The Origins of American Social Science* (Cambridge University Press, 1990), 300.

19. https://www.historians.org/about/aha-congressional-charter/ (visited May 12, 2025).

primarily on the Caribbean), translated sources on New Spain from archives in Mexico City and Sevilla, five volumes of legal cases related to slavery and four on the slave trade, and many more. Jameson liked to say that his work created the material that historians could deploy in ways they chose. He produced documentary collections that were like bricks, he said, which architects and builders used to construct their own edifices. Like the brick manufacturer, he was responsible for creating the material to be used, but not for the design or placement of the final product.[20]

Jameson also became an acute judge of fine scholarship. He had already edited the AHA's flagship journal, the *American Historical Review*, from its launch in 1895 until 1901. He had taken a hiatus from the journal while in Chicago, but he happily picked it up again as soon as he arrived in Washington in 1905. His editorship lasted for a record twenty-eight years. By the second decade of the twentieth century, Jameson was a powerful senior statesman of the field. He was part of a self-perpetuating elite inner circle that governed the AHA and the *AHR*. An annual gathering of a self-designated "Nucleus Club" met over a dinner (and champagne) and set all policy decisions in that jovial atmosphere. Jameson and his friend Frederick Jackson Turner were perennial figures in the Nucleus Club. Turner had been handpicked by Jameson as a loyal and trustworthy presence on the *AHR* editorial board, and given that both men were former AHA presidents, they had lifetime appointments to the executive council. The

20. Jameson to Henry Adams, October 31, 1910, in Donnan and Stock, *Historian's World*, 136.

journal had initially been unfunded: it was originally supported by twenty-six "guarantors," and it became the property of the board of editors, headed by Jameson.[21]

The inside-baseball quality of AHA governance set the
stage for pushback. The *Review*, in particular, turned away
most articles on the West and South; savvy younger historians now preferred the *Mississippi Valley Historical Review*
(the flagship journal of the Organization of American Historians, renamed the *Journal of American History* in 1964).
Jameson initially resisted any change, but he conceded eventually to moderate reform. He had been stunned when his
opponents demanded to see the AHA account books, which
were held by Jameson. And while they found no malfeasance,
Jameson was blasted for expensive meals, paid trips to meet-
ings for the Nucleus Club, and so on. But the rabble rous-
ers went too far, and at the December 1915 annual meeting,
a series of careful and limited reforms passed with virtually
unanimous acclaim. The *Review* became the responsibility of
the association. Every time Jameson's or Turner's name was
mentioned, the gathering cheered. "We hereby express our
full confidence in the men whose conduct and motives have
been thus impugned," said one loyalist to a roar of approval.[22]

21. Ray Allen Billington, "Tempest in Clio's Teapot: The American Historical Association Rebellion of 1915," *American Historical Review* 78, no. 2
(1973): 348–51.

22. Sidney B. Fay, "The American Historical Association," *The Nation*,
January 6, 1916, 22–23. Writing about the contretemps sixty years later, Ray
Allen Billington concluded that "Jameson was a superb editor who had made
the *Review* a model scholarly journal" and thus should never have been a tar-
get. It should be noted, however, that Billington's assessment of Jameson was
published in the *Review*. Billington, "Tempest in Clio's Teapot," 360.

Progressive leanings, together with deeply felt anti-populism, meant that Jameson and his friends and fellow travelers Frederick Jackson Turner, Woodrow Wilson, and others dedicated themselves to a thorough "contextual understanding of the past," as the scholar Dorothy Ross put it in her study of the development of social sciences in America.[23] The idea was to gather authoritative evidence that made possible the recovery of historical truths and the acquisition of genuine expertise. Jameson led the charge to discover, collect, catalogue, print, and examine manuscripts at home and abroad that had long slumbered in archives, many of which were based in Britain and Europe.[24]

The rigor of primary research was daunting. The effort that went into matching a vision of American exceptionalism with "scientific" (i.e., exhaustive and archivally driven) historiography required acrobatics that stymied most scholars. Frederick Jackson Turner's frontier thesis of the 1890s was the first and most influential effort to ground an admirable "American character" in its own history, rather than looking to Europe.[25] Meanwhile, Jameson was busily assembling material that would be folded into his lectures over the next thirty years, including those in the volume that is reprinted here.

23. Ross, *Origins of American Social Science*, 266.

24. Dixon Ryan Fox, *Herbert Levi Osgood: An American Scholar* (Columbia University Press, 1924), 67–83, 109–12, 122–33.

25. Frederick Jackson Turner, "The Significance of the Frontier in American History [1893]," in *The Frontier in American History* (Henry Holt and Company, 1920), 1–38.

As many historians have learned then and since, there is rarely an end to research: publication of historical scholarship represents an abandonment of the project as much as its completion. So, too, the struggle to square an ingrained commitment to democracy with an equally deep-seated dedication to the roles of expertise and centralized government was never ending. When Jameson relocated to the District of Columbia, he was enthused at the prospect of expanding historical expertise in the nation's capital, where government officials were beginning to understand the value of knowledge and training in rigorous scholarly disciplines, such as history. For these reasons, Jameson also played a leading role in the 1919 creation of the American Council of Learned Societies, which was headquartered in Washington and aimed to promote research across the humanities and social sciences. Founded in the wake of World War I, the organization's mission is to create and share knowledge "that advances understanding of humanity and human endeavors" and works "for a secure and peaceful world." But recovering the social and economic past in ways that both illustrated change over time and reinforced principles of good government was difficult, expensive, and specialized work. And the rumbles of populism meant that social history verged all too often on a threat to the progressive agenda that married historical expertise to administrative excellence and concentrated political power in Washington.[26]

---

26. Jameson, "Future Uses of History," 37–38. ACLS was the primary organization responsible for the *Dictionary of American Biography*, which was first published by Charles Scribner's Sons, under the "auspices" of the ACLS. A revamped project, still overseen by ACLS, has a new publisher and

Jameson's politics were generally those of a mildly conservative Progressive, one deeply invested in the social sciences and deference to expertise, rather than those of a social liberal. He supported Teddy Roosevelt and Woodrow Wilson. Across his lifetime, both Jim Crow and antisemitism grew in strength. He imagined himself swimming against these currents, declaring that he had none "of that race prejudice which I see to exist but cannot comprehend."[27] Yet he once disparaged a Jewish candidate for political office as "loud and vulgar." And when W.E.B. Du Bois objected to the *AHR*'s failure to capitalize the word "Negro" in his article on Reconstruction, Jameson replied that he was "astonished" that Du Bois would raise such an issue. He congratulated himself on being the "grandson of an old Abolitionist" and rejected the request.[28] Jameson was cautious, increasingly so as he witnessed the hardening of white supremacy, especially in Washington and even in his own family. In the early 1930s, Jameson's wife flatly refused to welcome into their home an accomplished Black researcher, Ruth Anna Fisher, whose talent was much admired by Jameson.[29]

---

a mission to include Black and Native Americans, immigrants, women, and "workers." "Preface," *American National Biography*, 24 vols. (Oxford University Press, 1999), 1:ii–v. https://www.acls.org/about/ (May 12, 2025).

27. Jameson to W.E.B. Du Bois, June 22, 1910, in Donnan and Stock, *Historian's World*, 133.

28. W.E.B. Du Bois, "Reconstruction and Its Benefits," *American Historical Review* 15, no. 4 (1910): 781–99; Jameson to W.E.B. Du Bois, June 22, 1910, in Donnan and Stock, *Historian's World*, 133.

29. August Meier and Elliott Rudwick, "J. Franklin Jameson, Carter G. Woodson, and the Foundations of Black Historiography," *American Historical Review* 89, no. 4 (1984): 1007.

But Jameson was also relentlessly committed to innovative research and scholarship, writing in 1917 that historians had "an imperative duty [to] make a far more thorough study of negro history than has hitherto been made." He solicited Du Bois's article on Reconstruction, which remained the only work by a Black author published in the *AHR* until John Hope Franklin's 1979 Presidential Address. Jameson also became an effective and dedicated supporter of Carter Woodson, founder of the Association for the Study of Negro Life and History in 1915. Woodson's obituary of Jameson, published in the *Journal of Negro History* in 1938, said that Jameson was neither "sentimental" nor manipulative. Working in a national capital defined by "racial autocracy," Jameson "did not have the courage" to hire a Black scholar at the Carnegie Institution, Woodson noted. But he was nevertheless a "great helper and faithful friend" to Black history and had been crucial in securing funding for the Association and its journal, writing letters and visiting leading foundations to urge them to support its work.[30]

Among Jameson's notable contributions while at the Carnegie Institute was the commissioning of two multivolume collections of documentary material, still in use by scholars, on the slave trade and on the legal history of race and slavery.[31] At a time when racist tropes and nostalgia for the

30. Jameson to George A. Plimpton, September 24, 1919, in Donnan and Stock, *Historian's World*, 243–44; Carter G. Woodson, "John Franklin Jameson," *Journal of Negro History* 23, no. 1 (1938): 131–33 The Association for the Study of Negro Life and History is now the Association for the Study of African American History and Life, https://asalh.org.

31. Elizabeth Donnan, ed., *Documents Illustrative of the History of the Slave Trade to America*, 4 vols. (Carnegie Institute of Washington, 1930–35);

Old South dominated much historical writing, Jameson championed these projects as the basis for an empirical, clear-eyed approach to the history of slavery. The sobering documents they contained, he wrote in 1926, reflected "not varieties of incident that *might* have presented themselves or could be imagined; they are records of actual happenings . . . when slavery prevailed in something like half of the United States."[32] Seen as a whole, Woodson concluded, Jameson's record made him "one of the greatest promoters" of Black history in an era when its white supporters were few.[33]

Jameson also developed a longstanding and profound interest in religious history—not just for its own sake and its influence on American history more broadly, but for its potential impact upon the present.[34] He argued that religious life in the United States was closely tied to the broader

Helen Tunnicliff Catterall, ed., *Judicial Cases Concerning American Slavery and the Negro*, 5 vols. (Carnegie Institute of Washington, 1926–37). Both series remain valuable research tools.

32. J. Franklin Jameson, "Preface," in Catterall, *Judicial Cases Concerning American Slavery and the Negro*, vol. 1, *Cases from the Courts of England, Virginia, West Virginia, and Kentucky* (Carnegie Institute of Washington, 1926), v.

33. Woodson, "John Franklin Jameson," 133. Ruth Anna Fisher, a longtime employee of Jameson, first as a collector of documents related to American history at the British Museum and Public Record Office and then at the Library of Congress, described obliquely Jameson's commitment to the study of race and slavery: his "imaginative suggestion . . . so far outstripped the thinking of his contemporaries as to lie dormant for several years." One of Jameson's greatest and most loyal admirers, Fisher was lead organizer for a festschrift published decades after Jameson's death. Fisher and Fox, *J. Franklin Jameson: A Tribute*, 8.

34. J. Franklin Jameson, "The American Acta Sanctorum," *American Historical Review* 13, no. 2 (1908): 286–302 (AHA presidential address), https://www.historians.org/presidential-address/j-franklin-jameson/.

social and political interests of the country, because "the affairs of the churches . . . have been managed by the laity or in accordance with their will . . . [and] reflected the mass of laymen." In his view, American history generally would be enriched by studying the "artless biograph[ies that memorialize ministers'] spiritual sufferings and triumphs [and inadvertently chronicle] . . . the lives of persons who exerted great and continuous influence on secular movements in their day and generation."[35]

Where Frederick Jackson Turner had stressed Americans' encounter with nature in his work on the frontier, Jameson gave religious life credit for Americans' resilience and intelligence. In particular, he argued that lay control of religious institutions was uniquely American, and that as a result, religious organizations were tied to democratic principles as well as virtue and ethics. As he put it in his fourth Princeton lecture, "religious freedom [and] equality" were the great (and linked) attributes of American civilization. The ministers who served these organizations were the individual heroes of the tale, servants of God just as Jameson was a servant of history.[36]

This version of American exceptionalism was as close as Jameson came to an argument for a defining thesis of American life, and it became the key theme in his AHA presidential address and reappeared in his lectures at Princeton. Yet Jameson never fleshed out this thesis in the full-throated way that would have been necessary to make such a claim resound as Turner's did. Instead, Jameson remained the

35. Jameson, "American Acta Sanctorum," 299.
36. Jameson, *American Revolution Considered as a Social Movement*, 90.

man behind the curtain, however evocative he found religious history. The centrality of religion to his understanding of American life has long hovered just out of sight of religious historians, but he was convinced that the study of religion was the most important and overlooked element in American historiography.

When the president of the Carnegie Institute declared that the organization would do better to fund only the physical (not the social) sciences because all "intelligent" people understood that "the physical sciences were of much greater utility to the development of the human mind than any others," Jameson fought back. Comparative religion, he argued, had done more "to improve the quality of European thinking . . . by the study of Oriental religions alone" than any advances in the physical sciences. Greater understanding and tolerance (as well as more effective administration of imperial colonies around the world) was the result. New work in linguistic, archeological, anthropological, and scriptural knowledge of religion was a great boon, said Jameson, considerably more useful than any scientific books "except one or two of Darwin's." Evolutionary biology, it bears noting here, focused on change over time, the central mandate of professional history.[37]

Jameson managed to defend his turf at the Carnegie Institute until a new president, John Merriam, arrived in

37. Jameson to Woodward, December 22, 1906, in Donnan and Stock, *Historian's World*, 102, 103. He also pointed to comparative legal knowledge as "educating the English in salutary ways." Henry Sumner Maine's *Ancient Law* (J. Murray, 1861), Jameson argued, was invaluable in refining British jurisprudence in India and other imperial settings. Donnan and Stock, *Historian's World*, 103.

1920. Merriam charged that Jameson had spent many years and significant sums without producing results. Unlike his own discipline (paleontology), Merriam said, Jameson and his historical department claimed to be following scientific principles but never drew conclusions. Instead, they demanded more and more evidence, constantly collecting but not controlling how the evidence was used by those who profited from their work. One must wait for the appearance of monographs based on the archival material he provided, Jameson had always believed, to be followed then by gradual writing of more synthetic histories.[38]

This work all took time (lots of time) and could not be hurried, Jameson maintained. It could be encouraged, but not controlled, because scholarship required so much expertise and diligence on the part of the historian. The results, however, would educate government officials, illuminating which practices would be successful and consistent with past events and the present flourishing of the country, especially in the growth of effective government. Making administrative agencies reflect the will of the people over time would allow the state to rise above politics. Only through such historical knowledge would government have the tools to work in the interest of all citizens. History gave its scholars the essential expertise to guide and improve administration,

---

38. Merriam's frustration with historians in general (and Jameson in particular) eventually led him to a plan for, as Jameson described it, "dissolving the Department to which I have given twenty-two years of labor." Jameson to Waldo Leland, November 9, 1927, Box 21, File "Jameson, J. Franklin, 1927," Waldo Gifford Leland Papers, Manuscript Division, Library of Congress (quoted in Rothberg, "Brahmin as Bureaucrat," 59).

the thinking went. Expertise, rather than politics or elections, would provide the material for exemplary statecraft. Jameson believed viscerally in this theory of history as key to good government. For him, the new scientific history was a national imperative.[39]

The relationship between historical scholarship and political life deepened in the Great War. Jameson entered the fray to support Woodrow Wilson and the war against Germany, hoping to match British scholars' *Oxford Pamphlets*. He organized a weekend gathering to discuss how historians could help the war effort, a goal that "presented itself to every history man in the country." He endorsed and supported publication of the Sisson Documents, a group of alleged top-secret memoranda, letters, and reports, bought in Russia by journalist Edgar Sisson. As a member of the Committee on Public Information, a propaganda machine of the Wilson administration, Sisson was positioned to stir the pot with sensational news and conspiracy theories. The Sisson Documents purported to show that Germany had financed the Russian Revolution and hired Lenin and Trotsky. Jameson and the University of Chicago Russian-language scholar Samuel Harper concluded that there was "no reason to doubt the genuineness or authenticity" of Sisson's collection. Just as American enthusiasm for the war against Germany ebbed in early 1918, Wilson published the documents as part of his successful campaign to rally support for the war effort.[40]

39. Ross, *Origins of American Social Science*, 278.

40. Jameson to Guy Stanton Ford, April 19, 1917, box 14, Guy Stanton Ford Papers, University of Minnesota, and Jameson to Robert Woodward, January 7, 1918, series 3, box 121, J. Franklin Jameson Papers, Library of Congress;

There were doubts about the documents when they were published, and the diplomat and historian George Kennan claimed in 1956 that he had proven their "extreme historical implausibility." The documents were "concocted," Kennan wrote, by a greedy forger, who peddled his wares to the British and the Americans. The British recognized that they were forgeries, but the Americans rose to the bait. Yet Kennan's attack was noted more by historians than the broader public. Persistent rumors that the Germans had indeed supported the Bolsheviks were confirmed by records found after World War II in Germany and in Soviet archives in the 1990s. The Sisson documents apparently were fabricated, but their plausibility, combined with pressure from Jameson (Kennan attacked him especially fiercely), helped put in motion unprecedented levels of propaganda, and a deepening alliance between the academy and President Wilson.[41]

Jameson also campaigned for an ongoing series of short (but learned) biographies of influential (and infamous) Americans, whose contributions might well otherwise go unnoticed. As Jameson pointed out, the *Dictionary of British National Biography* had established the benefits of calling attention to leading citizens, and any nation worth its salt should have a parallel publication. Such an undertaking

---

John Maxwell Hamilton, *Manipulating the Masses: Woodrow Wilson and the Birth of American Propaganda* (Louisiana State University Press, 2020), 175–80.

41. George Kennan, "The Sisson Documents," *Journal of Modern History* 28 (June 1956): 130–54; Les Adler and Thomas Paterson, "Red Fascism: The Merger of Nazi Germany and Soviet Russia in the American Image of Totalitarianism," *American Historical Review* 75, no. 4 (April 1970): 1046–64; Hamilton, *Manipulating the Masses*, 369–70.

was also expensive and time consuming, but Jameson was as determined as ever. Finally, in 1920, the wealthy Ochs family, publishers of the *New York Times*, agreed to fund the endeavor with a pledge of $50,000 per year for the next decade. The American Council of Learned Societies directed the project, then called the *Dictionary of American Biography*, which began publishing letter press volumes in 1928. The first edition of twenty volumes was completed in 1936 and featured some fifteen thousand biographies. Now known as the *American National Biography* and a valuable online resource for scholars, journalists, students, and more, it is still influential, although other sites, such as Wikipedia, have made inroads.[42]

Jameson left the Carnegie Institute in 1928, when he learned that its new director had plans to close his Department of Historical Research, the closest thing to a national historical commission that Jameson achieved in a lifetime of advocacy for such a group. The demise of his department and the reassignment of the institute's funds to the physical sciences were long in the works. But Jameson had fought gallant rearguard actions for almost his entire career, in his long battle to promote new support for historical research, lobbying and soliciting funds for costly projects, and defending the field from critics. His service was rewarded with a new job offer, which allowed him to pursue many of the goals he had long worked for, and to escape the increasingly hostile atmosphere of the Carnegie Institute.

42. See, e.g., "J. Franklin Jameson," Wikipedia, https://en.wikipedia.org /wiki/J._Franklin_Jameson.

Jameson was recruited as the first occupant of the newly endowed Benjamin Chair of American History and Chief of the Library of Congress Manuscript Division. The prior director's great interest was George Washington; his tenure had been distant and inactive. Jameson's first day saw him out and about among the staff, and his management style included detailed knowledge of everyone's projects and duties, steady expansion of the number of employees, and ensuring that they made progress. As one employee put it, "we all worked harder for him than we would have worked for any supervisor he might have interposed."[43]

At the Library of Congress, Jameson was empowered to collect valuable documents for research, rather than reproducing those held in other archives. As Jameson assumed the new post, he planned to maintain "close relations with the members of the historical profession, who have so heartily supported my past endeavors, and perhaps to do some useful things not yet attempted." His acquisitions included the papers of Woodrow Wilson and the manuscript of the autobiography of Abraham Lincoln, to give just two examples. His relationships also paved the way for future acquisitions. His support for the work of Carter Woodson eventually brought Woodson's collection of manuscripts in Black history to the Library of Congress.[44]

Jameson had long advocated for the establishment of a national archive for the United States. In 1907, he met with

43. Curtis W. Garrison, "Dr. Jameson's Other Side: A Personal Memoir," in Fisher and Fox, *J. Franklin Jameson: A Tribute*, 58.

44. Jameson to Henry O. Taylor (then President of the AHA), November 9, 1927, in Donnan and Stock, *Historian's World*, 326–27.

President Theodore Roosevelt, who granted him access to all executive branch records, so that he might estimate how much space would be needed for an archive. Starting in 1911, Jameson recruited political support among progressive Congressmen, published articles in *The Nation*, and even persuaded the American Legion, which was horrified at the condition of military records, to endorse the project. Congress awarded $5,000 in 1913 for the design of an archives building, and plans were completed in 1916. Then the long campaign for funding construction began, which eventually drew endorsements from the American Library Association and the Daughters of the American Revolution.[45] Hearst newspapers and the *Washington Herald* ran many stories about the poor condition of federal records in the early 1920s, and finally the building was authorized in the Public Buildings Act of 1926. The National Archives opened officially in 1937, the year of Jameson's death, but the appointment in 1934 of the first National Archivist, Robert D. W. Connor of North Carolina, put a Jameson protégé in charge of the institution that he had fought for tirelessly for decades.[46]

Jameson died in 1937, going to work at the Library of Congress until the very end of his days. Fittingly, his biography was included in a 1950s supplement to the *Dictionary*. It was written by Waldo Leland, who had worked with Jameson first at the Carnegie Institute and then at the Manuscript Division, and who was deeply involved with the

45. Victor Gondos Jr., *J. Franklin Jameson and the Birth of the National Archives, 1906–1926* (University of Pennsylvania Press, 1981).

46. Fred Shelley, "The Interest of J. Franklin Jameson in the American National Archives, 1908–34," *American Archivist* 12, no. 2 (1949): 129.

American Council of Learned Societies from its founding in 1919 through the end of World War II. As one might expect, the biography is learned and balanced, if uncritical. Leland was one among many young historians whose careers were supported and steered by Jameson. Always ready to welcome a new and promising entrant in the field, Jameson's generally austere demeanor veiled a generous nature and wry sense of humor. He was a loyal and often lifelong friend, whose mentorship nurtured the research and monographs of dozens of historians. A slim volume published in the mid-1960s included reminiscences of those who were indebted to Jameson (and still alive). Jameson's readiness "to give countenance to ambitious young men," the journalist and historian Allan Nevins wrote in his tribute, thinking back to a much younger version of himself, had been "a prime element in [Jameson's] zeal for the invigoration of historical work."[47]

Indeed, Jameson combined a reserved and even withdrawn character with great generosity of spirit. His mien tended toward the more formal, even stiff, end of the spectrum. Each summer during the last twenty years of his life, Jameson hosted an exclusive "convivium historicum" for pedigreed historian friends and allies at a seaside resort in Branford, Connecticut. "A large part of the time," one attendee later recalled, "was spent in rocking chairs on the piazza, generally gathered about an austere-looking gentleman . . . who

47. Leland, "Jameson, J. Franklin." A second Jameson biography, this time by Morey Rothberg, was published in 1999. https://doi-org/10.1093/anb/9780198606697.article.1400317 (May 12, 2025). Allan Nevins, "The Sage and the Young Man," in Fisher and Fox, *J. Franklin Jameson: A Tribute*, 42.

sat very erect and discoursed, ex cathedra and in very precise English, about the multitudinous problems of the historian." Even his admirers conceded that the initial impression was one of reserve, and he did not suffer fools gladly. One protégé described his criticism as "shattering," another called him "austere," a third called him "inordinately shy" in ways that were often misunderstood as critical. But he was also "inspirational," "affectionate," "generous," "patient," and "dignified." Jameson's dedication to the field of history made him a sought-after advisor to young entrants to the field, whose work he quite rightly saw as the most important element of a growing field.[48]

Some called Jameson "patrician," even a "Boston Brahmin" and a "Puritan." None of these labels were accurate, however. Jameson was influential, and (mildly) snobbish, but had nowhere near the wealth or connections of a Brahmin, and Puritans had been extinct for well over a century before Jameson was born. His family teetered on the brink of (and sometimes fell into) poverty. Jameson attended public schools as a boy (in comparison with elite Bostonians, whose sons were often tutored at home until they left for boarding schools at about age ten), and his father's loss of the Amherst postmaster position in 1884 was devastating for the family.

48. Conyers Read, review of *An Historian's World: Selections from the Correspondence of John Franklin Jameson*, ed. Elizabeth Donnan and Leo F. Stock, *Pennsylvania Magazine of History and Biography* 80, no. 4 (October 1956): 513; Young and Nobles, *Whose American Revolution Was It?*, 22; Fisher and Fox, *J. Franklin Jameson: A Tribute*, 3, 4 (Ruth Anna Fisher), 43 (Allan Nevins), 46 (Mary Dearing), 55 (Curtis W. Garrison), 98 (David Mearns); Jameson to Daniel C. Gilman, February 14, 1902, in Donnan and Stock, *Historian's World*, 80.

Perhaps because he had seen such hardship in his own family, Jameson valued knowledge about and appreciation for everyday people. His great gift lay in his ability to build and nurture historical scholarship and in supporting those who undertook such work.[49]

Given the breadth of Jameson's efforts at building the scaffolding of the field—all historians in the United States and many beyond are still beneficiaries—one might expect his scholarly output would be negligible. Indeed, Jameson himself conceded that he had never produced a transformative work, like those written by Turner, Nevins, Beard, Bemis, and others. His own efforts were dedicated to assembling the tools of history. Yet one might argue that the lectures he gave late in his career demonstrated his power to inspire scholars to ask new questions. One hundred years later, many historians consider Jameson a social historian before his time, but rarely are his great efforts to build the field even mentioned. Jameson's renown as the founder of the central institutions of the profession, in other words, was long outlived by the

49. Scholars have repeatedly invoked the Brahmin description, with some acknowledgment that doing so requires sharp departure from the standard definition of the term. But Jameson was born in working-class Somerville, attended public schools, had no distinguished ancestors or connections (his uncle was a grocer, his grandparents also storekeepers in Woburn, not the home of Brahmins!), married a schoolteacher, and his family became increasingly impoverished over time. Equally telling, Jameson's Scotch-Irish ancestry meant a Presbyterian (rather than a Congregationalist or Episcopalian) religious upbringing. Nor did Jameson interact on a regular basis with Boston Brahmins. See, e.g., Rothberg, "Brahmin as Bureaucrat," 49; Garrison, "Dr. Jameson's Other Side," in Fisher and Fox, *J. Franklin Jameson: A Tribute*, 56 ("patrician"), 48 ("Brahmin"); Young and Nobles, *Whose American Revolution Was It?*, 23 ("Brahmin"); "Jameson," *American Historical Review*, 244 ("Puritan").

slim volume presented here. *The American Revolution Considered as a Social Movement* was a game changer.

Jameson's published lectures made a powerful case for opening a new dimension in the study of the American Revolution, a field long dominated by nationalist histories of revolutionary politics and the military conflict. He had been thinking and speaking about the Revolution as a social movement since 1895, when he lectured on the subject at Barnard College. His arguments remained largely unchanged when he delivered a revised version of the lectures at Princeton in 1925 and published them the following year.[50] Jameson was not the first to address the Revolution's social history in print; by 1926, Charles Beard, Carl Becker, and Arthur Schlesinger Sr. had all made important forays into the economic history of the Revolution (especially the role of merchant wealth) and its internal fissures.[51] But Jameson's lectures were national in scope, and through his four capacious organizing themes—status, land, commerce, and belief—they investigated a wide range of the

50. Morey Rothberg, "John Franklin Jameson and the Creation of *The American Revolution Considered as a Social Movement*," in *The Transforming Hand of Revolution: Reconsidering the American Revolution as a Social Movement*, ed. Ronald Hoffman and Peter J. Albert (University Press of Virginia, 1995), 1–26. This volume grew out of a 1989 symposium by the same name.

51. Carl Becker, *The History of Political Parties in the Province of New York, 1760–1776* (University of Wisconsin, 1909); Charles A. Beard, *An Economic Interpretation of the Constitution of the United States* (The Macmillan Company, 1913); Arthur M. Schlesinger, *Colonial Merchants and the American Revolution, 1763–1776* (Columbia University, 1918).

Revolution's social consequences. His fellow Progressive historians had jump-started a monographic literature, but Jameson was the first to offer a view from ten thousand feet.

In the ensuing years, the significant impact of Jameson's little book was not reflected in its sales, despite a glowing review by Beard in *The New Republic*. In its first twenty-seven years, *The American Revolution Considered as a Social Movement* sold only 1,356 copies—an average of fifty per year.[52] Nevertheless, the book became a cornerstone of the field. During the 1930s and '40s, historians of the Revolution took up many of the themes Jameson had touched upon: land policy and loyalist confiscation, church history, business history, intellectual history, and the status of slavery and indentured servitude. By the early 1950s, scholars regarded the book as "a landmark in recent American historiography" and quipped that it "had been cited in all textbooks and monographs for a generation."[53] In the preface to an affordable thirtieth-anniversary paperback edition released by Beacon Press in 1956, Schlesinger Sr. called its initial publication "an epoch-marking if not epoch-making event" in American historical scholarship, a book that embodied a turn toward seeing "the American past as embracing all the concerns and activities of the people."[54]

Even as it was elevated to the status of a scholarly classic and rereleased in search of a wider readership, though,

52. Beard, "Challenge to Windbags," 344; W. Stull Holt, "Who Reads the Best Histories?," *Mississippi Valley Historical Review* 40, no. 4 (1954): 615–17.

53. Frederick B. Tolles, "The American Revolution Considered as a Social Movement: A Re-Evaluation," *American Historical Review* 60, no. 1 (1954): 1; Holt, "Who Reads the Best Histories?," 619.

54. Schlesinger, introduction to Jameson, *American Revolution Considered as a Social Movement* (Beacon Press, 1956), x.

Jameson's book and the intellectual concerns it represented were eclipsed by a rapidly evolving historiography. Jameson himself had encouraged the comparative study of revolutions, musing in his first lecture about a "natural history of revolutions."[55] In the mid-twentieth century, as American politics and diplomacy were roiled by the legacies of foreign revolutions with much more transformative social content— the Russian Revolution (which Jameson had briefly noted in 1926), the Communist Revolution in China, the Cuban Revolution—the American Revolution's social consequences looked comparatively smaller, until it seemed like not much of a social movement at all. Rather, it assumed the shape of an intellectual and constitutional event: moderate, consensual, legalistic, largely bloodless, and accompanied by incremental social change. At the height of the Cold War, scholars who shared Jameson's commitment to a usable democratic past abandoned the Progressives' search for historical conflicts. Now, they celebrated and emphasized the degree of consensus in American history. In the study of the American Revolution in particular, historians turned from social questions toward the study of ideas and republican ideology. They also shifted their attention to the origins of the Revolution and away from its more fractious consequences. If scholars such as Edmund and Helen Morgan, Robert E. Brown, and Bernard Bailyn sought to disprove the Progressive interpretation of the founding, though, they did not attack Jameson so much as dismiss him—preferring instead to engage with

55. Jameson, *American Revolution Considered as a Social Movement* (Princeton University Press, 2025), 8, 10.

other targets, such as Beard, whose arguments and writings they took more seriously.[56]

The new social historians and New Left historians of the 1960s and 1970s inherited Jameson's conviction that the American Revolution was a transformative event socially as well as politically. Their historical methods and their own politics, though, could hardly have been more different than his. New Left historians such as Jesse Lemisch, Staughton Lynd, and Alfred Young sought to reinterpret the founding era "from the bottom-up," revealing how ordinary people had experienced and influenced the Revolution. Jameson's lectures had depicted society as a whole organism or an assemblage of regions, communities, and interests, and when he referred to or quoted individuals, they were typically educated elites. The New Left historians, by contrast, were interested in recovering the experiences and voices of ordinary people who Jameson had seen mainly *en masse*: farmers, tenants, sailors, artisans, laborers. They were also far more willing than he had been to see the social history of the revolutionary era through the prism of class.[57]

---

56. Edmund Morgan and Helen Morgan, *The Stamp Act Crisis: Prologue to Revolution* (University of North Carolina Press, 1953); Robert E. Brown, *Middle-Class Democracy and the Revolution in Massachusetts, 1691–1780* (Cornell University Press, 1955); Edmund Morgan, *The Birth of the Republic, 1763–1789* (University of Chicago Press, 1956); Bernard Bailyn, *The Ideological Origins of the American Revolution* (Harvard University Press, 1967).

57. For instance: Staughton Lynd, "Who Should Rule at Home? Dutchess County, New York, in the American Revolution," *William and Mary Quarterly* 18, no. 3 (1961): 330–59; Jesse Lemisch, "Jack Tar in the Streets: Merchant Seamen in the Politics of Revolutionary America," *William and Mary Quarterly* 25, no. 3 (1968): 371–407; Alfred F. Young, "George Robert Twelves Hewes

At the same time, a second, partially overlapping group of historians pioneered more quantitative methods for the study of daily life and social transformation. These "new social historians" were inspired by the *Annales* school, a French historiographical movement that looked past the froth and churn of political events to investigate economic and social trends over the *longue durée*. Turning to long-ignored sources such as tax lists and vital records, social historians of early America tended to aim their questions not at concentrated periods of revolutionary upheaval but rather at longer stretches of time and more gradual, structural change. Some of them, however, in the tradition of Jameson, sought to connect social analysis to the narrative of political events. Landmark studies by Gary Nash, Robert Gross, and others asked how social factors shaped political consciousness and the causes and course of the American Revolution.[58]

To a significant degree, this quest—to identify the social changes of the revolutionary era, and to uncover their relationships to colonial resistance, patriot rebellion, and the creation of an independent republic—mirrored many of the questions raised by Jameson and has driven scholarship in the field ever since. From the era of the Civil Rights movement, the Vietnam War, second-wave feminism, and the US Bicentennial to the present, this challenge has been continually renewed by expanding notions of what counts as social transformation

---

(1742–1840): A Boston Shoemaker and the Memory of the American Revolution," *William and Mary Quarterly* 38, no. 4 (1981): 561–623.

58. Robert Gross, *The Minutemen and Their World* (Hill and Wang, 1976); Gary Nash, *The Urban Crucible: Social Change, Political Consciousness, and the Origins of the American Revolution* (Harvard University Press, 1979).

and whose stories matter for understanding the American Revolution. In 1973, for instance, John Shy urged historians to attend to the transformative effects of the Revolutionary War itself upon society, downgrading the army and its generals, and stressing the ubiquity of the militias and their role as agents of social and political change. In 1980, monumental books by Linda Kerber and Mary Beth Norton opened a debate about whether and how the Revolution changed the status of women. Ethnohistorians drew scholarly attention to Native American participation in the Revolution, tracing its social consequences across cultures. Building on the pioneering work of Benjamin Quarles, and spurred in part by Edmund Morgan's wrenching account of the "central paradox" of slavery and freedom in the nation's colonial origins, scholars began recovering the revolutionary experiences of African Americans and examining more thoroughly the Revolution's consequences for race and slavery as social institutions—new histories that would, in turn, transform interpretations of revolutionary politics.[59]

Through the kind of archival empiricism that Jameson championed, these scholars investigated how Americans of

59. John Shy, "The American Revolution: The Military Conflict Considered as a Revolutionary War," in *Essays on the American Revolution*, ed. Stephen G. Kurtz and James H. Hutson (University of North Carolina Press, 1973), 121–56; Linda Kerber, *Women of the Republic: Intellect and Ideology in Revolutionary America* (University of North Carolina Press, 1980); Mary Beth Norton, *Liberty's Daughters: The Revolutionary Experience of American Women, 1750–1800* (Little, Brown, 1980); Colin G. Calloway, *The American Revolution in Indian Country: Crisis and Diversity in Native American Communities* (Cambridge University Press, 1995); Benjamin Quarles, *The Negro in the American Revolution* (University of North Carolina Press, 1961); Edmund Morgan, *American Slavery, American Freedom: The Ordeal of Colonial Virginia* (Norton, 1975).

all sorts experienced the Revolution. Their research yielded new insights into the *how* and the *why* behind the Revolution's unintended social consequences, which Jameson himself in 1926 could only attempt to capture through metaphor: "the stream of revolution" overflowing its banks, the "transforming hand of revolution" upending social institutions. But their findings also pointed in myriad new directions. The explosion of early American social history was accompanied by—and indeed made possible by—increased scholarly specialization. By the late twentieth century, some historians yearned for a new synthesis, the kind of synoptic view Jameson had been able to offer back when the monographic literature on the American Revolution could fit on a single shelf.[60]

That is what Gordon Wood sought to provide in his controversial *The Radicalism of the American Revolution* (1991). Claiming the mantle of Jameson in the book's opening pages, Wood offered a sweeping account of social transformation. The Revolution, he argued, supplanted traditional monarchy and aristocracy with a society and government that championed the interests of ordinary people, inadvertently but inexorably creating the United States' egalitarian, capitalist democracy. This, for Wood, represented no less radical a revolution than France's or Russia's.[61]

In making this argument, however, Wood largely ignored the previous two decades of research into the complexity and diversity of early American society. If the Revolution radically rewired American society around democratic individualism

60. Jameson, *American Revolution Considered as a Social Movement*, 7, 8.
61. Gordon S. Wood, *The Radicalism of the American Revolution* (Knopf, 1991), 5–6.

and equality, this was true only for a minority of the population. As Michael Zuckerman put it in one particularly memorable critique, Wood's *Radicalism* "denies class at every turn," "disregards race, gender, and ethnicity almost entirely," and "has shrunk America to a country without slaves, women, families, or the South." Critics also found it tough to pin down causes in Wood's interpretation, or even whether the social transformations he described had much to do with the struggle for US independence. Despite its eloquence and detail, many scholars found *Radicalism* unpersuasive, and neither more concrete nor more inclusive than Jameson's initial inquiry into the Revolution's social consequences. In its achievements and its flaws, Wood's book recharged the field—often as not (and in marked contrast to the impact of Jameson's lectures) because young historians defined their own scholarly agendas against it.[62]

Several years after *Radicalism* appeared, in an exhaustive historiographical essay, Alfred Young used Jameson's 1926 book to organize a panoramic survey of the field's key debates and evolution from the Progressives to Gordon Wood. Young's article was longer than Jameson's published lectures themselves, and its message was clear: Jameson's questions continued to orient the study of the American Revolution, and the agenda he had framed seventy years prior remained far from complete.[63]

62. Michael Zuckerman, "Rhetoric, Reality, and the Revolution: The Genteel Radicalism of Gordon Wood," *William and Mary Quarterly* 51, no. 4 (1994): 697–98.

63. Alfred F. Young, "American Historians Confront 'The Transforming Hand of Revolution,'" in Hoffman and Albert, *Transforming Hand of Revolution*, 346–492. Young's essay was reprinted in Young and Nobles, *Whose American Revolution Was It?*, 13–133.

On the cusp of the semiquincentennial, the Revolution's social dimensions remain the subject of vibrant new scholarship. But recent work investigates social transformations of a very different sort from those that occupied Jameson's (and Wood's) attention. Where Jameson's Revolution pushed society "in the direction of levelling democracy," historians today are more apt to see a Revolution defined by inequality, exclusion, and violence. Beyond a colonial independence movement or the creation of an American republic, new histories view the Revolution as, variously, a vicious civil war, a slave revolt, a massive disruption in household relations, a financial frenzy, a shock to religious life, and a settler uprising. Its social consequences included not just egalitarian sentiments and expanding opportunity, but also economic unrest, dispossession, displacement, and newly virulent forms of racial prejudice.[64]

What unites much of this new scholarship is a renewed focus on the military struggle itself. Although it was long deemphasized in social and intellectual histories alike, historians today are "bringing the war back in" to the study of the American Revolution. They are uncovering the disorder that military occupation and wartime vengeance wrought upon households and communities. They are exploring political strategies for wartime mobilization that instilled racial prejudice at the heart of American nationhood and society. They are reframing the Revolutionary War as a settler-colonial contest

---

64. Two recent syntheses reinterpret the revolutionary era along these lines: Alan Taylor, *American Revolutions: A Continental History, 1750–1804* (Norton, 2016); Woody Holton, *Liberty Is Sweet: The Hidden History of the American Revolution* (Simon & Schuster, 2021).

for land and illuminating its profound implications for Native American sovereignty and societies.[65]

In 1926, J. Franklin Jameson broke new ground in the study of the Revolution by encouraging scholars to look past the generals and battles. It is perhaps an ironic measure of his book's enduring impact that, a century later, some of the freshest social perspectives on the Revolution are coming from historians who are returning our attention to the military struggle. Examining the war's transformative effects upon society, these scholars are yielding powerful new insights into what was (and wasn't) truly revolutionary about the American Revolution.

{⟨⟩⟨⟩}

The American Revolution Considered as a Social Movement is a curious classic. The fruit of decades of research, the book does not announce itself as a feat of archival discovery (it contains no footnotes). It brims with fresh insights, but it is not a masterwork of historical argument: the structure of its analysis is more associative than cumulative. Although lucid, engaging, and occasionally witty, it does not stand out as a

65. See, for instance, Kathleen Duval, *Independence Lost: Lives on the Edge of the American Revolution* (Random House, 2015); Robert G. Parkinson, *The Common Cause: Creating Race and Nation in the American Revolution* (University of North Carolina Press, 2016); Donald F. Johnson, *Occupied America: British Military Rule and the Experience of Revolution* (University of Pennsylvania Press, 2020); Katherine Carté, *Religion and the American Revolution: An Imperial History* (University of North Carolina Press, 2021); T. Cole Jones, *Captives of Liberty: Prisoners of War and the Politics of Vengeance in the American Revolution* (University of Pennsylvania Press, 2020); Lauren Duval, *The Home Front: Revolutionary Households, Military Occupation, and the Making of American Independence* (University of North Carolina Press, 2025).

literary achievement. Jameson's voice is expository and scientific rather than narrative or lyrical. It is exceedingly rare for any work, especially a published set of lectures, to become such a staple of scholarly citations and graduate-school reading lists. Why, then, has this slim volume stood the test of time?

Perhaps the book's longevity is best explained by the style of its interpretation—its posture toward readers. Easily read in one sitting, *The American Revolution Considered as a Social Movement* is nonetheless expansive. It touches on a wide array of topics without trying to be definitive on any of them. It is neither strident nor dogmatic. Instead, Jameson's historical curiosity drives it forward. Progressing gently from topic to topic, the book feels more like a nature walk than a treatise.

Critics have for decades argued that this ambulatory quality (even vagueness) means that Jameson was not a serious historian. They have a point, but so did Jameson. He invited readers to draw connections, ask questions, see patterns. Behind the book's account of social transformation lies a more fundamental claim: the Revolution was not only one or even two things; rather, it unleashed and sustained a dizzying multiplicity of effects. This broadening impulse licenses new perspectives, encouraging readers to write the field's next chapter. In short, this little book offered a set of opportunities and challenges for subsequent historians to take up as their own. In that sense, *The American Revolution Considered as a Social Movement* was an institution-builder, in the spirit of its author.

Michael A. Blaakman and
Sarah Barringer Gordon

THE AMERICAN REVOLUTION
CONSIDERED AS A SOCIAL MOVEMENT

The Revolution and
the Status of Persons

In this year 1925 we enter upon a long series of celebrations commemorating the one hundred and fiftieth anniversaries of the successive events of the American Revolution. If any of those present are able, like myself, to remember well the long series of centennial commemorations of those same events that marked the years from 1875 to 1883, and even to 1889, they will, I think, agree with me that those celebrations did more than anything else that has happened in our lifetime to stimulate popular interest in American history in general, and specifically in the history of the American Revolution. The *Magazine of American History* was founded at once, in 1876. The Daughters of the American Revolution, a more numerous body than ever before were united in the commemoration of any portion of history, and the two societies of Sons, date from that period. A still wider, though indirect, indication of popular historic interest may be seen in the passion for what is called "colonial" furniture, a passion which distinctly flowed from these commemorations and especially from the Philadelphia Centennial of 1876, for it is certain that down to that year the sway of black walnut and funereal horsehair was steadily maintained. A less popular but more fruitful blossoming of interest in history may be seen in the striking rapidity with which, in the 'eighties immediately succeeding, professorships of history were established in the American colleges and universities, and in the sudden zeal with which numbers of able young students devoted themselves to the study of their country's history.

The consequences which flowed from the celebrations of fifty years ago are so far certain to repeat themselves in our time that we may at least be sure of a speedy heightening of interest in the history of the American Revolution. The main desire that has underlain the preparation of the ensuing lectures has been the wish that whatever results, whether in learned academic research or in popular thinking, may spring from this new period of commemorations, may be marked by a wider view of the events than was taken fifty years ago. Surely it ought to be so, in view of the advances which history has made in America in fifty years, from a time when there were probably not a dozen professional students of history in the United States to a time when there are at least several hundreds.

The gain, the wider view, should show itself in three ways. In the first place, it ought to be possible for us to be much fairer to the British or Loyalist opponents of our fathers than were the men of fifty years ago. They had hardly emancipated themselves from the traditional view, generated in the heat of the old conflict, that the British statesmen of that time were monstrous tyrants, the British soldiers monstrous barbarians. There is, to be sure, an opinion abroad that the permanent maintenance of that view is an essential trait of American patriotism. It is conceded that in the study of every other war—of Athens against Sparta, or Rome against Carthage, or Parliamentarian against Royalist, or Prussia against France, or Union against Confederacy—it is the duty of rational beings to hear both sides, and not to suppose that the ultimate truth of history is to be gathered by listening solely to the immediate war-cries of one of the two contestants. An historical student who has no special affection for England, but on the other hand is not seeking any office for which he needs Irish-American votes, cannot help raising in some perplexity the question why the common-sense rules of fairness should be inapplicable to this war alone among all wars, why our histories of it should be sedulously guarded against improvement, or why writers who take a modern and detached view of it should be accused of the covert reception of British gold.

Another advance that we ought to make consists in a revision of the popular estimate of the men of Revolutionary times. Fifty years ago, and even a hundred years ago, there had become fixed in the public mind the notion that, because in the period of the Revolution there were many heroic characters and deeds, the whole American population of that time was heroic. It is pleasant to think well of a whole generation of those who have preceded us, and especially pleasant to glorify them if they were our ancestors. It may seem harmless, but when it is done in terms of comparison with later generations it is not altogether wholesome. It is not wholesome because it is not just. Nothing can be more certain than that, if we consider the whole nation and not merely the individual instances of heroic character and conduct, the patriotism of 1861, on both sides, was much more widely extended and more ardent than the much-lauded patriotism of 1776, and that of 1918 more pervasive, more enlightened, and more pure than either. How could we expect it to be otherwise, when we consider carefully the circumstances of the time? Let us distinguish between the heroes who fought and suffered and made every sacrifice to bring into existence a new nation, and the population at large, of whom so great a proportion were, as a matter of fact, however we may excuse them, provincial-minded, dubious in opinion, reluctant to make any sacrifices, half-hearted in the glorious cause. All honor to the heroes, and they were many.

> We sit here in the Promised Land,
>> That flows with Freedom's honey and milk;
> But 'twas they won it, sword in hand,
>> Making the nettle danger soft for us as silk.

But let us not forget that a large part of their heroism had to be expended in overcoming difficulties which need not have existed but for the slackness and indifference of their fellows. For instance, no episode of the history of the Revolution affords a finer example of patriotic sacrifice than the winter's encampment at Valley Forge; but why were the sufferings at Valley Forge encountered? Simply because the country at large, with whatever excuses, did not support the war, and the army which was waging it, with any approach to the ardor which was shown in 1861, on both sides, or in 1918. Clothes and shoes and blankets and tents were lacking. Who does not know what would happen if an American army of the present day were found to be destitute even of chocolate drops? It would not be three days before the metropolitan dailies would be voicing loudly a nation's wrath, and car-loads of chocolate drops would be rushed promptly to every camp. Let us be fair to the moderns, and not fabricate an imaginary golden age in the undeveloped America of 1776.

Thirdly, and closer to the immediate purpose of these lectures, it is to be wished that in the coming commemorations and in our future thinking we may consider the American Revolution in broader aspects than simply the political and the military. Fifty years ago, it was these that engrossed attention, and indeed most that has been written since then about the Revolution has been narrowly confined to these two aspects, the political and the military, including of late the naval. Every move in the political struggle for independence from Great Britain, every action of the Continental Congress, has been described over and over again. Every battle and every skirmish in that long and dragging war has had its historian, or has been the theme of meticulous articles or controversial pamphlets. Meanwhile, even in this age when social history is so much in fashion all over the world, few writers have concerned themselves with the social aspects of our American revolutionary history.

How different is it with the Frenchmen's study of the great French Revolution! Forty or fifty years ago they were in much the same state as we: every move of the politicians, every picturesque happening in Paris, every march or engagement of the revolutionary armies, was eagerly chronicled by intelligent but more or less conventional historians; but in more recent years the horizon of the French historians of their revolution has broadened, and more attention has been given to the prodigious effects of the French Revolution upon the constitution of French society than to the political events, more to the march of the revolutionary ideas than to the march of the revolutionary battalions, and quite as much to the progress of the revolution in the provinces as to the dramatic events that marked its development in Paris. The result has been that the French Revolution is now seen in its true proportions and effects, not simply as the downfall of monarchy or the securing of equal political rights for all individuals, but chiefly as a social movement, French and European, of vast dimensions and of immense significance.

Perhaps some may be moved to say at once: But this is precisely to ignore the most salient contrast between the American Revolution and the French. The men of our Revolution, they will say, were neither levellers nor theorists. Their aims were distinctly political, not social. They fought for their own concrete rights as Englishmen, not for the abstract rights of man, nor for liberty, equality, and fraternity. The French rose in revolt against both a vicious political system and a vicious social system. With enthusiastic ardor they proceeded to sweep away abuses of all sorts, and to create, not simply a new government, but a new France and indeed, to their own imaginations, a new heaven and a new earth. That they cared more for the social than for the political results of the Revolution was evident when, after a few years, believing it impossible to retain both, they resigned political freedom and threw themselves into the arms of the young Corsican who gave promise of preserving for them their new social system. Not so, it will be said, the Anglo-Saxon. He had no wish to destroy or to recast his social system. He sought for political freedom, but he had no mind to allow revolution to extend itself beyond that limited sphere. As Burke said, he was "taught to look with horror on those children of their country who are prompted rashly to hack that aged parent to pieces and put him into the kettle of magicians, in hopes that by their poisonous weeds and wild incantations they may regenerate the paternal constitution."

It is indeed true that our Revolution was strikingly unlike that of France, and that most of those who originated it had no other than a political programme, and would have considered its work done when political independence of Great Britain had been secured. But who can say to the waves of revolution: Thus far shall we go and no farther? The various fibres of a nation's life are knit together in great complexity. It is impossible to sever some without also loosening others, and setting them free to combine anew in widely different forms. The Americans were much more conservative than the French. But their political and their social systems, though both were, as the great orator said, still in the gristle and not yet hardened into the bone of manhood, were too intimately connected to permit that the one should remain unchanged while the other was radically altered. The stream of revolution, once started, could not be confined within narrow banks, but spread abroad upon the land. Many economic desires, many social aspirations were set free by the political struggle, many aspects of colonial society profoundly altered by the forces thus let loose. The relations of social classes to each other, the institution of slavery, the system of landholding, the course of business, the forms and spirit of the intellectual and religious life, all felt the transforming hand of revolution, all emerged from under it in shapes advanced many degrees nearer to those we know.

These are only assertions. They cannot be adequately proved in a few lectures. It will content the lecturer if he can partially illustrate their truth, and if some who hear him are convinced that here is a field of history deserving further and deeper study. Meantime we might profitably consider for a moment whether it is intrinsically probable that our revolution was unlike other popular revolutions, in having no social results flowing from the political upheaval. Is there such a thing as a natural history of revolutions? Nation differs from nation, and age from age, but there are some uniformities in human nature, some natural sequences recurrently presenting themselves in human history. Not all political revolutions, it is true, have had important social consequences. One notable variety of revolution is that whereby one reigning individual or one small group of individuals holding supreme power is supplanted by another individual or small group, without any serious alteration of the system. Such are those "palace revolutions" whereby Jehu the son of Nimshi succeeds Jehoram the son of Ahab, or the tsar Alexander supplants the tsar Paul, without more disturbance of the social system than when "Amurath to Amurath succeeds" in a wholly peaceable manner. But it is the other variety, popular revolutions, which we have in mind. This is the variety which figures most largely in modern history. A popular revolution usually consists in the transfer of political power from the hands of a smaller into those of a larger mass of the citizens, or from one great section of the population to another. As the result of such a revolution, we expect to see the new group exercising its new-found power in accordance with its own interests or desires, until, with or without fixed intention of so doing, it alters the social system into something according better with its own ideals. After the peaceful English revolution known as the passing of the Parliamentary Reform Act of 1832, we look to see the new Parliament, chosen by a wider suffrage and representing now the middle classes, passing a mass of legislation that brings the social state of England into better conformity with middle-class ideals. After the American Civil War, which shifted the seat of political power from the planting aristocracy of the South to the manufacturing and commercial classes of the North, we look to see legislation and the growth of custom whereby the American social system takes on forms congenial to the minds of the new possessors of power. But indeed we do not need to look farther into the past than the last nine years, to observe how the greatest of all revolutions, the one destined evidently to be the most momentous in its consequences, beginning with the overthrow of a tsar and the substitution of a republic, speedily escapes from the control of those who would keep it purely or mainly political, and transforms Russian society by 1925 to an extent which no one would in 1913 have dreamed to be possible.

If then it is rational to suppose that the American Revolution had some social consequences, what would they be likely to be? It would be natural to reply that it depends on the question, who caused the Revolution, and that therefore it becomes important to inquire what manner of men they were, and what they would be likely, consciously or unconsciously, to desire. In reality, the matter is not quite so simple as that. Allowance has to be made for one important fact in the natural history of revolutions, and that is that, as they progress, they tend to fall into the hands of men holding more and more advanced or extreme views, less and less restrained by traditional attachment to the old order of things. Therefore the social consequences of a revolution are not necessarily shaped by the conscious or unconscious desires of those who started it, but more likely by the desires of those who came into control of it at later stages of its development.

You know how it was with the English Revolution of the seventeenth century. At first it was the affair of moderate statesmen, like Pym and Hampden, or moderate generals like Essex or Manchester, earls, who would not push the king too hard, but before long it fell into the hands of men like Cromwell, whose spirit is shown by his bold declaration, "If I should meet the king in battle, I would as soon fire my pistol at him as at any man." Now when we examine the interesting mass of constitutional and social legislation enacted by the parliaments of the Commonwealth, we see in it the work of men of far more advanced views than those of Pym and Hampden, to wit, of radicals who had come into control of the movement in its latest stages.

Or again, take the French Revolution. Everyone knows how its history is marked by distinct successive periods, in each of which the control is exercised by a group more radical and extreme than its predecessors; and the same has been true of the great Russian Revolution. Now, widely as our American Revolution differed from these, do not let us suppose that it escaped every trait of conformity to the natural history of such movements. Certain it is that, in some of our states at least, it fell ultimately into quite other hands than those that set it in motion.

Well, then, we may ask, who were in favor of the Revolution, and who were against it? The answer of course varies with the different stages of its development. In 1774 the partisans of American independence were very few, though there had long been those who thought, in an academic way, that it would soon take place. In most years after 1776 the partisans of American independence were the great majority. But what sort of man became a Tory as it gradually became necessary to take sides? What sort of man became a Whig? As a matter of course, almost all persons who enjoyed office under the Crown became Tories, and these were a large number. In an age when the king's turnspit was a member of Parliament, and under a king whose chief means of political action was the distribution of offices, officeholders were certain to be numerous, and their pay was, in proportion to the wealth of the country and the work they had to do, much greater than it is now. If the natural desire of all mankind to hold on to a lucrative office (a desire which is said sometimes to influence political action even in this age) did not make an officeholder a Tory, there was another motive arising from the fact that he had been appointed and had sworn to execute the laws, and might therefore feel in duty bound to obey the instructions, of the ministers in England. As for the merchants, many, who had extensive interests that were imperilled by rebellion, adhered to the royal cause. But on the whole the great body of the merchants of the thirteen colonies were Whigs, for of the deep underlying causes, which for a generation had been moving the American mind in the direction of independence, none was so potent, according to all the best testimony, as the parliamentary restrictions on the trade of the colonies. Among farmers many of the richest took the royalist side. Probably most Episcopalians did so, except in the South. Everywhere the debtor class was, as was natural, and as has been true the whole world over, mainly on the side of revolution.

If we speak of professions, we should note that probably most of the clergy were Whigs, with the exception of nearly all the clergymen of the Church of England in the northern colonies. Most lawyers were Whigs, but most of the most eminent and of those enjoying the largest practice were Tories. John Adams says that, of the eight lawyers who had an important practice before the Superior Court of Massachusetts at the time of the Stamp Act, only Otis and he were Whigs ten years later. One of the others had died, and the remaining five were Tories. Among physicians the proportion of Tories was quite as large as among lawyers.

A word as to race and nationality. Colonists who had very recently arrived from England were likely to take the Tory side. Immigrants from Scotland, also, were usually Tories. A hundred and fifty years ago the Scots at home were among the warmest of Tories; Hume's *History of England* is typical of their feelings. Perhaps, too, their well-known clannishness gave them, in America, the position of aliens who held together, and would not assimilate with the rest of the population. Of the Irish, on the other hand, and those of the Scotch-Irish stock, Protestants from the north of Ireland, it is customary to hold that they were warmly and by vast majority on the side of revolution. It is not so certain. Industrious efforts have been made to show that they formed the backbone of the Revolutionary army—efforts partly based on a misinterpretation of a single passage in Joseph Galloway's testimony before a committee of the House of Commons. On the other hand, I have observed that, in the two large lists of Loyalist claimants that give the country of birth, 146 out of 1358 claimants, or eleven per cent, say that they were born in Ireland—a larger number than were born in England. Yet in Pennsylvania, where the proportion of Irish or Scotch-Irish population was greatest, it was unquestionably their influence that carried the state for independence, at the same time breaking the power in state affairs of the Philadelphia conservatives, and bestowing upon the state a radically democratic constitution. In all the colonies the Germans generally adhered to the party of independence, but not with great ardency.

As is usually the case, the revolutionary side was more frequently espoused by young men, the conservative cause by their elders. There were not a few conspicuous cases, such as that of Sir John Randolph, the king's attorney-general in Virginia, and his son Edmund Randolph, in which the son adopted the former, the father the latter cause, and other cases, like that of Samuel and Josiah Quincy, in which an elder and a younger brother were thus divided. Among all the leaders of the Revolution, very few were forty-five years old in 1775; most were under forty. But think for a moment of the leaders of the French Revolution—Robespierre thirty-one years old when the Revolution began, Danton thirty, Camille Desmoulins twenty-seven, Collot-d'Herbois thirty-nine, Couthon thirty-three, Lebas twenty-four, Saint-Just twenty-one—and we shall see cause to be glad that our Revolution was carried through by men who, though still young, had at any rate reached their full maturity of thought and of character.

If we should investigate the Tory party in the several colonies in detail, we should be forced to the conviction that, in New England, it comprised in 1775 a very great share, probably more than half, of the most educated, wealthy, and hitherto respected classes. In March 1776, when Howe evacuated Boston, eleven hundred refugees sailed away with him. These eleven hundred, and the thousand or more who subsequently followed them, bore away perhaps a majority of the old aristocracy of Massachusetts. The act of banishment which the state legislature passed in 1778, to punish the Tories, includes among its three hundred-odd names some representatives of most of the families which had been distinguished in the earlier days of the colony. The loss of this important element, cultivated, experienced, and public-spirited, was a very serious one. It is true that many Tories returned after the war, but their fortunes were usually much broken, and they could never regain their influence. In New England, in short, it appears that the Revolution brought new strata everywhere to the surface.

In New York it seems probable that, in the height of the war at least, the bulk of the property-owners belonged to the Tory party, and it was strong also among the middle classes of the towns and among the country population. On the large manorial estates the tenant farmers sided with their landlords if they took sides at all. The city of New York and the county of Westchester were strongly Tory during at least the period of the British occupation, and Westchester very likely before. So were Staten Island and the three counties of Long Island.

In Pennsylvania it is probable that during the critical years of the war, at least, the majority of the population was on the side of the Crown, and that majority seems to have included many persons of eminence, and many Quakers. On the other hand, as is well known, the Virginian aristocracy in general, living somewhat remote from the influence of the royal officials, upon their secluded estates, were full of the spirit of local independence. Quite unlike their New England compeers, they took the Whig side, and that almost unanimously. It was the Virginian planters who formed the local committees, seized from the outset the control of the movement, and made it impossible for loyalty to show itself in concerted or effective action. And it is well known how numerous and active were the Tories in the Carolinas. But, says Dr. Ramsay, speaking of South Carolina, "Beside their superiority in numbers, there was an ardour and enthusiasm in the friends of Congress which was generally wanting in the advocates for royal government." Is not this a most significant touch? After all the evidence as to classes and numbers—for perhaps there were a hundred thousand Loyalist exiles, to say nothing of the many more who did not emigrate—the ultimate success of the American cause might well seem to us a miracle. But the fact remains that the Revolutionary party knew what they wanted. They had a definite programme, they had boldness and resolution, while those averse to independence were divided in their counsels, and paralyzed by the timidity which naturally cleaves to conservative minds. The first scientific observer of political revolutions, Thucydides, pointed out, and every subsequent revolution has accentuated his words, that in such times boldness and energy are more important requisites to success than intelligence or all other qualities put together. This is the secret of the whole matter. "There was an ardour and enthusiasm in the friends of Congress which was generally wanting in the advocates for royal government."

All things considered, it seems clear that in most states the strength of the revolutionary party lay most largely in the plain people, as distinguished from the aristocracy. It lay not in the mob or rabble, for American society was overwhelmingly rural and not urban, and had no sufficient amount of mob or rabble to control the movement, but in the peasantry, substantial and energetic though poor, in the small farmers and frontiersmen. And so, although there were men of great possessions like George Washington and Charles Carroll of Carrollton who contributed a conservative element, in the main we must expect to see our social changes tending in the direction of levelling democracy.

It would be aside from the declared purpose of these lectures to dwell upon the political effects which resulted from the victory of a party constituted in the manner that has been described. There are, however, some political changes that almost inevitably bring social changes in their wake. Take, for instance, the expansion of the suffrage. The status in which the electoral franchise was left at the end of the Revolutionary period fell far short of complete democracy. Yet during the years we are considering the right of suffrage was much extended. The freeholder, or owner of real estate, was given special privileges in four of the new state constitutions, two others widened the suffrage to include all owners of either land or personal property to a certain limit, and two others conferred it upon all tax-payers. Now if in this lecture we are considering especially the status of persons, we must take account of the fact that the elevation of whole classes of people to the status of voters elevates them also in their social status. American society in the colonial period had a more definite and stable organization than it ever has had since the Revolution. It had been like that English county society of which the poet speaks,

> Where Aylmer followed Aylmer at the hall,
>   And Averill Averill at the rectory.

Now, multitudes of squires had been driven into exile or dethroned from their high position of dominance over the community. Multitudes of other Loyalists had been disfranchised, or impoverished by confiscations. Rip Van Winkle, whose sleep bridged just these years, found the atmosphere of his village radically altered. Jeremy Belknap of New Hampshire, writing in 1792, after remarking on the effect of the Revolution in calling the democratic power into action and repressing the aristocratic spirit, confesses that in the new state "the deficiency of persons qualified for the various departments in the Government has been much regretted, and by none more than by those few who know how public business ought to be conducted." In that entertaining Virginian autobiography, the *Life* of the Reverend Devereux Jarratt, after speaking of the habit in that writer's youth, among the plain people with whom he grew up, of regarding gentlefolk as beings of a superior order, he says in 1794:

> But I have lived to see a vast alteration in this respect and the contrary extreme prevail. In our high republican times there is more levelling than ought to be, consistent with good government. I have as little notion of oppression and tyranny as any man, but a due subordination is essentially requisite in every government. At present there is too little regard and reverence paid to magistrates and persons in public office; and whence do this regard and irreverence originate but from the notion and practice of levelling? An idea is held out to us that our present government and state are far superior to the former, when we were under the royal administration; but my age enables me to know that the people are not now by half so peacefully and quietly governed as formerly; nor are the laws, perhaps by the tenth part, so well executed. And yet I know the superiority of the present government. In theory it is certainly superior; but in practice it is not so. This can arise from nothing so much as from want of a proper distinction between the various orders of the people.

Similar voices come from North Carolina, where one stout conservative laments the "extension of that most delicate and important right [of suffrage] to every biped of the forest," and another declares that: "Anyone who has the least pretence to be a gentleman is suspected and borne down *per ignobile vulgus*—a set of men without reading, experience, or principle to govern them." In fact, the sense of social change pervaded the country. A writer in South Carolina says, quite in the spirit of these lectures, "There is nothing more common than to confound the terms of the American Revolution with those of the late American war. The American war is over, but this is far from being the case with the American revolution. On the contrary, nothing but the first act of the great drama is closed."

The workings of the popular sentiment in favor of equality may of course be plainly seen in the legislation abolishing rights of primogeniture and distributing more or less equally the estates of persons dying intestate, but this movement may perhaps be more conveniently considered in a lecture devoted to the Revolution and the Land. We might also expect the equalitarian or humane spirit to show itself in alterations of the laws respecting redemptioners or indented servants. Those laws, however, seem not to have been changed in the Revolutionary period. We may infer that the laws protecting the interests of such persons, a very numerous class in the years just preceding the Revolution, either were, or were deemed to be, adequate already for their humane purpose, and that the status of the indented, who after all had but a few years to serve and then would have all the rights of other poor people, was not regarded as seriously unsatisfactory.

A far more serious question, in any consideration of the effect of the American Revolution on the status of persons, is that of its influence on the institution of slavery, for at this time the contrast between American freedom and American slavery comes out, for the first time, with startling distinctness. It has often been asked: How could men who were engaged in a great and inspiring struggle for liberty fail to perceive the inconsistency between their professions and endeavors in that contest and their actions with respect to their bondmen? How could they fail to see the application of their doctrines respecting the rights of man to the black men who were held among them in bondage far more reprehensible than that to which they indignantly proclaimed themselves to have been subjected by the King of Great Britain?

At the time when the Revolution broke out there were about a half-million of slaves in the Thirteen Colonies, the figures probably running about as follows: 200,000 in Virginia, 100,000 in South Carolina, 70,000 or 80,000 each in Maryland and in North Carolina, 25,000 perhaps in New York, 10,000 in New Jersey, 6,000 in Pennsylvania, 6,000 in Connecticut, 5,000 in Massachusetts, 4,000 in Rhode Island. Slavery in the continental colonies at that time was no doubt less harsh than in the West Indies, and milder than it has been in many other countries and times. An English parson, preaching to a Virginian congregation in 1763, says: "I do you no more than justice in bearing witness, that in no part of the world were slaves ever better treated than, in general, they are in the colonies." But slavery is slavery, and already before the Revolution many hearts had been stirred against it. It is of course true that other influences than those of the American Revolution were abroad in the world at the same time which would surely work in some degree against the institution of human slavery. On the one hand Voltaire had raised a powerful, if at times a grating, voice in favor of a rational humanitarianism, and Rousseau had poured upon

time-worn institutions the active solvent of abounding senti-
mentality. Quite at another extreme of human thought from
them, Wesley and Whitefield had stirred the English nation
into a warmth of religious feeling of which Methodism was
only one result, and with it came a revived interest in all varieties of philanthropic endeavor.

There is no lack of evidence that, in the American world of
that time, the analogy between freedom for whites and freedom for blacks was seen. If we are to select but one example
of such evidence, the foremost place must surely be given to
the striking language of Patrick Henry, used in 1773, when
he was immersed in the struggle against Great Britain. It is
found in a letter which he wrote to one who had sent him a
copy of Anthony Benezet's book on slavery.

> Is it not amazing [he says] that at a time, when the rights
> of humanity are defined and understood with precision,
> in a country above all others fond of liberty, that in such
> an age and in such a country we find men professing a
> religion the most humane, mild, gentle and generous,
> adopting a principle as repugnant to humanity as it is
> inconsistent with the Bible and destructive to liberty? ...
> Would anyone believe I am the master of slaves of my own
> purchase! I am drawn along by the general inconvenience
> of living here without them. I will not, I can not justify it.
> However culpable my conduct, I will so far pay my devoir
> to virtue, as to own the excellence and rectitude of her pre-
> cepts, and lament my want of conformity to them. I believe
> a time will come when an opportunity will be offered to
> abolish this lamentable evil. Everything we can do is to

improve it, if it happens in our day, if not, let us transmit to our descendants, together with our slaves, a pity for their unhappy lot, and an abhorrence of slavery. . . . It is a debt we owe to the purity of our religion, to show that it is at variance with that law which warrants slavery.

Along with many examples and expressions of individual opinion, we may note the organized efforts toward the removal or alleviation of slavery manifested in the creation of a whole group of societies for these purposes. The first anti-slavery society in this or any other country was formed on April 14, 1775, five days before the battle of Lexington, by a meeting at the Sun Tavern, on Second Street in Philadelphia. The members were mostly of the Society of Friends. The organization took the name of "The Society for the Relief of Free Negroes unlawfully held in Bondage." In the preamble of their constitution they point out that "loosing the bonds of wickedness and setting the oppressed free, is evidently a duty incumbent on all professors of Christianity, but more especially at a time when justice, liberty, and the laws of the land are the general topics among most ranks and stations of men." The New York "Society for Promoting the Manumission of Slaves" was organized in 1785, with John Jay for its first president. In 1788 a society similar to these two was founded in Delaware, and within four years there were other such in Rhode Island, Connecticut, New Jersey, Maryland, and Virginia, and local societies enough to make at least thirteen, mostly in the slave-holding states.

In actual results of the growing sentiment, we may note, first of all, the checking of the importation of slaves, and thus of the horrors of the trans-Atlantic slave trade. The Continental Congress of 1774 had been in session but a few days when they decreed an "American Association," or non-importation agreement, in which one section read: "That we will neither import nor purchase any slave imported after the first day of December next, after which we will wholly discontinue the slave trade, and will neither be concerned in it ourselves, nor will we hire our vessels nor sell our commodities or manufactures to those who are concerned in it"; and the evidence seems to be that the terms of this agreement were enforced throughout the war with little evasion.

States also acted. Four months before this, in July 1774, Rhode Island had passed a law to the effect that all slaves thereafter brought into the colony should be free. The influence under which it was passed may be seen from the preamble. "Whereas," it begins, "the inhabitants of America are generally engaged in the preservation of their own rights and liberties, among which that of personal freedom must be considered as the greatest, and as those who are desirous of enjoying all the advantages of liberty themselves should be willing to extend personal liberty to others," etc. A similar law was passed that same year in Connecticut. Delaware prohibited importation in 1776, Virginia in 1778, Maryland in 1783, South Carolina in 1787, for a term of years, and North Carolina, in 1786, imposed a larger duty on each negro imported.

Still further, the states in which slaves were few proceeded, directly as a consequence of the Revolutionary movement, to effect the immediate or gradual abolition of slavery itself. Vermont had never recognized its existence, but Vermont was not recognized as a state. Pennsylvania in 1780 provided for gradual abolition, by an act which declared that no negro born after that date should be held in any sort of bondage after he became twenty-eight years old, and that up to that time his service should be simply like that of an indented servant or apprentice. Now what says the preamble of this act? That when we consider our deliverance from the abhorrent condition to which Great Britain has tried to reduce us, we are called on to manifest the sincerity of our professions of freedom, and to give substantial proof of gratitude, by extending a portion of our freedom to others, who, though of a different color, are the work of the same Almighty hand. Evidently here also the leaven of the Revolution was working as a prime cause in this philanthropic endeavor.

The Superior Court of Massachusetts declared that slavery had been abolished in that state by the mere declaration of its constitution that "all men are born free and equal." In 1784 Connecticut and Rhode Island passed acts which gradually extinguished slavery. In other states, ameliorations of the law respecting slaves were effected even though the abolition of slavery could not be brought about. Thus in 1782 Virginia passed an act which provided that any owner might, by an instrument properly attested, freely manumit all his slaves, if he gave security that their maintenance should not become a public charge. It may seem but a slight thing, this law making private manumission easy where before it had been difficult. But it appears to have led in eight years to the freeing of more than ten thousand slaves, twice as great a number as were freed by reason of the Massachusetts constitution, and as many as there were in Rhode Island and Connecticut together when the war broke out.

That all was not done that might have been done for the removal or amelioration of slavery we cannot deny, nor that there was in many places a glaring contrast between the principles avowed by the men of the Revolution and their acts respecting slavery; yet very substantial progress was made, and that more was made in this period than in any other until a much later time may be taken as clear evidence of a pronounced influence of the Revolution upon the status of persons in the realm where that status stood most in need of amelioration.

Thus in many ways the successful struggle for the independence of the United States affected the character of American society by altering the status of persons. The freeing of the community led not unnaturally to the freeing of the individual; the raising of colonies to the position of independent states brought with it the promotion of many a man to a higher order in the scale of privilege or conse- quence. So far at any rate as this aspect of life in America is concerned, it is vain to think of the Revolution as solely a series of political or military events.

II

The Revolution and
the Land

It would appear from the satirical remarks of Dickens and others that, eighty years ago, the first question asked of a European visitor to any part of the United States was, "How do you like our institutions?" Our institutions, especially the institutions of democracy, were thought of as the most notable possession or attribute of the United States, and many indeed seem to have regarded them as the source of all our prosperity and prospects of advancement.

But during the past fifty years historians have not been idle, and, though it runs counter to many contemptuous or patronizing declarations that I see in print, to me they seem to have been doing their work with a certain degree of intelligence. In particular, they have been much impressed with the thought that the average man, in all ages, has been more occupied with making a living than with any other one thing.

This has led them to doubt whether economic phenomena are not more often the cause than the effect of political institutions and arrangements, and in the case of American history to question closely the view that our political institutions are the source from which all blessings flow.

The doctrine which underlies the present lecture is that political democracy came to the United States as a result of economic democracy, that this nation came to be marked by political institutions of a democratic type because it had, still earlier, come to be characterized in its economic life by democratic arrangements and practices. We do not look to see effects precede causes, and certainly political democracy came among us somewhat late, certainly long after the Revolution in most states. If we take manhood suffrage as the most convenient symbol of political democracy, we have to say that it was 1840 before manhood suffrage came at all close to being the universal rule of American political life. Long before this, however, America stood committed to economic democracy, which meant, in a country so occupied with agriculture, to the system of landholding which the classical economists called "peasant proprietorship," the system of small holdings where landowner, capitalist or farmer, and laborer are all one, the owner of the land supplying the capital and working the fields with his own labor and that of his family.

It is difficult for us now to imagine a country so entirely rural as was the America of a hundred and fifty years ago. The population was sparse, but that does not tell the whole story. There are parts of the country now, even in the regions east of the Mississippi, that are thinly settled. But none of them lies outside the sphere of influence of a large city, and most of them have cities and large towns near at hand. Almost half of our whole vast population dwells in towns of more than 8,000 inhabitants. Now when the Revolution began there were in all the thirteen colonies but five towns of that size, and only two or three per cent of the people lived in them. From the pastures of Maine to the rice-fields of Georgia, America was almost absolutely rural, and her people were almost wholly devoted to agriculture. We hear much of the commerce, the fisheries, and the manufactures of New England. Dr. Franklin, some years after the war, declared roundly that these occupations did not engross the time and capital of more than a tenth as many New Englanders as were occupied with agriculture. Much more in other colonies must it have dominated all other pursuits. If this be so, it needs no demonstration that the relations of the American to the land were of the very first consequence. Therefore, in our study of the social changes which accompanied and followed upon the American Revolution, we may properly give a place of great prominence to the land. Is there indeed any portion of American history in which we get far away from that primary relationship? "Land," was the first cry of the wave-tossed mariners of Columbus; land-hunger among the crowded inhabitants of western Europe was the chief impulse toward the colonization of the New World; and in all times till quite lately the chief task of American manhood has been this, to go up against the land and possess it, to subdue the continent, to win for mankind its primary victory over the elemental forces of nature. Under what forms of organization these battles should be won was of the first consequence to the future of the country and of the world. Naturally, the first attacks were made under forms derived from the Old World. Chartered companies were given extensive grants of the soil. Lords of the council, whom spendthrift monarchs had not the means to reward properly in England for zealous services to the Crown, were appeased by vague grants of territories in the American wilderness. It was all so unknown that the grants might perchance overlap each other, but there was probably something over there out of which a courtier could make something. Hence those strange paraphernalia of palatines and landgraves and admirals and chamberlains and chancellors with which the proprietors of Carolina decorated and burdened their infant province—"thrones, dominions, principalities, and powers," but few inhabitants. Elsewhere, perhaps, manors were erected, with courts baron and courts leet and all the machinery of English estates. Upon the Hudson River the Dutch West India Company established patroons, with almost regal rights over great feudal principalities, so extensive as quite to overshadow the settlements of lesser folk.

But if we bring up before our minds the familiar map of the Atlantic portions of the United States, we see at a glance that there was a marked difference between the physical geography of the northern and the southern regions of that coast. In the north the mountains and the foot-hills that spread out before them come close to the sea, and the rivercourses are troubled, but a few miles back from the coast, by rapids and waterfalls. Here, therefore, the settler, if he would have a market in those days of water-transportation, must live near the sea. The soil, too, uneven and unfertile, was such as could be profitably worked only by one who gave his personal attention to a small area of it. Here, therefore, compact settlement was the rule, and large estates were likely to be the exception—that is to say, large estates of cultivated land, for there was nothing to make it difficult for one man to hold great tracts of forest, or wild lands of the interior. But as one goes southward the mountains recede from the coast. The alluvial belt grows broader. Long navigable rivers penetrate the country, such as those which divide Virginia into long and narrow peninsulas. Here the English immigrant could indulge to the full his natural English propensity toward a large estate of land and a life properly separated from that of his fellows. All around his home, too, the land lay in great levels which could profitably be managed upon a large scale and by the labor of hired servants or slaves. While, then, New England had few large estates, and its aristocracy was chiefly urban, throughout the rest of the country the English system of large properties was extensively followed. There were large manors in New York and Pennsylvania and Maryland, estates embracing thousands of acres each in Virginia and the colonies farther southward. The manorial grants in New York embraced more than two and a half million acres. In 1769 it was estimated that at least five-sixths of the inhabitants of Westchester County lived within the confines of the great manors there, and the great Van Rensselaer manor, a hundred miles farther up the Hudson, covered an area of twenty-four miles by twenty-eight, two-thirds the size of Rhode Island. The Fairfax estate in Virginia at one time embraced six million acres; that of Lord Granville in North Carolina included at least a third of the colony.

But all this was, as has been hinted, a European system transplanted to the New World. It was not native here, and in some respects it was not natural, nor well suited to American conditions of life. It would do very well for certain alluvial districts of the Atlantic region, but it would not do at all for the broad belt of hilly and mountainous country which lay next to the westward. Yet to attack that uneven region and subdue it to the purpose of man was the next task which lay before the eager and indomitable American spirit. The English system of land-tenure had well enough served the uses of America thus far, perhaps, but it would not serve them much longer. Its hold upon America was loose. If anything should occur which should administer a great shock to the entire social system of the country, it would dislodge and shake off from the body politic, as an outworn vesture, such institutions as no longer met our needs. Now this is just what the Revolution did. It broke up so much that was traditional and customary with the Americans, in dissolving their allegiance to a monarchy for which they had felt a most loyal attachment, that whatever else was outgrown or exotic seemed to be thrown into the melting-pot, to be recast into a form better suited to the work which the new nation had before it. The hot sun of revolution withered whatever was not deeply rooted in the soil. There was no violent outbreak against the land-system, for there had been no grinding oppressions or exactions connected with it. No maddened and blood-stained peasants rushed furiously from château to château, burning court-rolls and shedding the blood of seigneurs and châtelains. But in a quiet, sober, Anglo-Saxon way a great change was effected in the land-system of America between the years 1775 and 1795.

In the first place, royal restrictions on the acquisition of land fell into abeyance. The king's proclamation of 1763, forbidding settlement and the patenting of lands beyond the Alleghenies, and those provisions of the Quebec Act of 1774 which in a similar sense restricted westward expansion and the formation of new, interior colonies had, it is true, never been executed with complete rigidity, but they, and the uncertainties of the months preceding the war, had certainly checked many a project of large colonization and many a plan for speculation in land. Now these checks were removed. Moreover, all the vast domains of the Crown fell into the hands of the states, and were at the disposal of the state legislatures, and it was certain that these popular assemblies would dispose of them in some manner that would be agreeable to popular desires. Whether the land law in respect to old holdings should be altered by the Revolution or should remain unchanged, it was certain that in respect to new lands, on which the future hopes of American agriculture and settlement rested, a more democratic system would be installed.

Then there was the matter of the quit-rents, which in most of the colonies, according to the terms on which lands were granted to individual occupants, were to be paid to the crown or to the proprietary of the province. They ranged from a penny an acre to a shilling a hundred acres per annum. It is true that payment was largely evaded, but since the amount received at the time when the Revolution broke out was nearly $100,000, we may count the quit-rent as something of a limitation upon the ready acquisition of land. So at any rate the colonists regarded it, for in making their new constitutions and regulations respecting lands they abolished quit-rents with great emphasis and vigor, and forbade them for the future.

Another encumbrance on land-tenure which the Revolution removed was the provision, by British statute intended to ensure an adequate supply of masts for the royal navy, that no man should cut white-pine trees on his land till the king's surveyor of woods had surveyed it and designated the trees, sometimes many in number, which were to be reserved for the king's use. It is true that the law was not rigorously enforced; it could not be, with such staff as the surveyors had. But John Wentworth, the last royal governor of New Hampshire and the last surveyor of the king's woods in New England, tried diligently to enforce it, and, though he did it tactfully, he found it everywhere exceedingly unpopular. With the coming of the Revolution, the restriction came to an end, and fee simple was fee simple.

In the fourth place, great confiscations of Tory estates were carried out by the state legislatures, generally in the height of the war. New Hampshire confiscated twenty-eight estates, including the large property of its governor, Sir John Wentworth. In Massachusetts a sweeping act confiscated at one blow all the property of all who had fought against the United States or had even retired into places under British authority without permission from the American government. Among the lands confiscated by special mention were those of Sir William Pepperrell, the second baronet of that name, whose vast estate in Maine extended so far along the coast that it was said he could ride all the way from Kittery Point to Saco, a distance of thirty miles, on his own land. In New York, all lands and rents of the crown and all estates of fifty-nine named persons were confiscated, the greatest among them, probably, being that of the Phillipse connection. Probably something like three hundred square miles of the old Phillipse estates were confiscated, bearing a value of several hundred thousand dollars. By 1782 the state of New York had confiscated royalist property in land valued at $2,500,000 in hard money. In all, the state probably received $3,150,000 Spanish dollars for forfeited real estate.

The largest estate confiscated was that of the Penn family, proprietaries of Pennsylvania, which they estimated at nearly a million pounds sterling. The commissioners of the state of Maryland who sold confiscated property in that state took in more than £450,000 sterling. In Georgia the single estate of Sir James Wright was valued at $160,000. The broad lands of the sixth Lord Fairfax, the genial old man in whose service Washington had first practised as a surveyor, and those of Sir John Johnson in the Mohawk country, 50,000 acres, are other examples of Tory confiscation on the grand scale. In one colony and another, hundreds of estates were confiscated. Altogether, it is evident that a great deal of land changed hands, and that the confiscation of Tory estates contributed powerfully to break up the system of large landed properties, since the states usually sold the lands thus acquired in much smaller parcels. Thus the New York law discouraged the sale of such lands in parcels of more than 500 acres. James De Lancey's real estate went to 275 persons, Roger Morris's to 250. A general idea of the extent of the confiscation may be gained from the fact that the British Parliament, after every effort to reduce the claims of the Loyalists, finally compensated them with grants aggregating over three million pounds sterling. To be sure, this was for both real and personal estate, but on the other hand it is to be said that the

Loyalists themselves estimated the value of their claims upon Mr. Pitt's government as high as eight million pounds.

These Tory confiscation acts, by the way, had one curious effect upon the development of American institutions. There is no American institution more famous, none that has excited more comment in other countries, largely erroneous comment, to be sure, than the power of American courts to set aside laws for want of conformity to the Constitution. It is often spoken of as a peculiar power of the United States Supreme Court and as a peculiar invention of those who made the Constitution of 1787. In reality it is a power or duty of any court acting under a written constitution, and it was exercised in several instances by state courts before there was a Supreme Court of the United States and before the Constitution of 1787 was framed. It so happens that in most of these cases the law against which this objection was raised was a law regarding Tories. The legislatures were so hot against the Tories and so eager in the pursuit of their spoils that they quite overstepped constitutional bounds in their enactments against them. Among the lawyers there grew up the idea, virtually a new idea, that courts might set aside laws if they conflicted with the constitution of the state. The fact is, I suppose, that during this period the legislatures were in the hands of the radical revolutionaries, or extreme Whigs, while the lawyers and judges were more moderate and conservative members of that party.

But to return to the laws dealing with land alone. If, as I have suggested, nothing was more important in the American social system than its relation to the land, and if the Revolution had any social effects at all, we should expect to see it overthrowing any old-fashioned features which still continued to exist in the land laws. What, then, was the old land-law in the American colonies? The feudal ages had discovered that, if men desired to give stability to society by keeping property in the hands of the same families generation after generation, the best way to do this was to entail the lands strictly, so that the holder could not sell them or even give them away, and to have a law of primogeniture, which, in case the father made no will, would turn over all his lands to the eldest son, to the exclusion of all the other children. There could not be two better devices for forming and maintaining a land-holding aristocracy. When the Revolution broke out, Pennsylvania and Maryland had abolished primogeniture, and South Carolina had abolished entails. But in New York, New Jersey, Virginia, North Carolina, and Georgia, entails and primogeniture flourished almost as they did in old England. Indeed, Virginian entails were stricter than the English. The New England colonies had a peculiar rule of their own for the descent of land in case a man left no will. They liked a democratic distribution, and yet they could not feel quite comfortable to cut away entirely from the old English notions about the eldest son. Moreover, their Puritanical feeling for the law of Moses (Deut. xxi. 17) was very strong. Accordingly, they arranged that in such a case all the children should inherit equally, except that the eldest son should have a double share. Then came the Revolution. In ten years from the Declaration of Independence every state had abolished entails excepting two, and those were two in which entails were rare. In fifteen years every state, without exception, abolished primogeniture and in some form provided for equality of inheritance, since which time the American eldest son has never been a privileged character. It is painful to have to confess that two states, North Carolina and New Jersey, did not at once put the daughters of the Revolution upon a level with the sons. North Carolina for a few years provided for equal distribution of the lands among the sons alone, and not among daughters save in case there were no sons. New Jersey gave the sons a double share. But elsewhere absolute equality was introduced. Now I submit that this was not an accident. How hard Washington found it to get these thirteen legislatures to act together! And yet here we find them all with one accord making precisely the same changes in their land-laws. Such uniformity must have had a common cause, and where shall we find it if we do not admit that our Revolution, however much it differed from the French Revolution in spirit, yet carried in itself the seeds of a social revolution? Democratic land-tenure was the natural thing in a new country like America, and made its way at once when political revolution loosened the ties of old habit.

It seems impossible to form any secure judgment as to the total amount of land set free, or brought into a more democratic form of landholding, by all this state legislation, but there can be no question that the change was of large extent, and had extensive social consequences. In the largest of the colonies, it is estimated by the highest authority that Mr. Jefferson's act of 1776 released from entail at least half, and possibly three-quarters, of the entire "seated" area of Virginia. An act of 1705 had forbidden the docking of entails by fine and common recovery. Thenceforward an act of the legislature was necessary in order to release an estate from entail, and the pages of Hening, from that time to the Revolution, show many such enactments. But those acts seldom operated permanently to release from the practice of entail the lands to which they applied, for the new purchaser usually created a new estate tail. Moreover, the prosperous eighteenth century planter, living on an old estate in the tidewater region but ever acquiring new lands in the back country, most commonly entailed his acquired lands upon his younger sons, while passing on his inherited estate, under an old entail, to the eldest.

Social democracy and political democracy progressed together in the legislation of the Revolutionary period respecting the suffrage, for before the Revolution the electoral franchise was largely based on land. In the colonial times the right to vote had nowhere been very narrowly restricted, but in all the colonies there had been a property qualification, usually amounting to $150 or $250. In six of the colonies it had been necessary to own real estate, no amount of personal property sufficing. In the northern colonies the real estate usually fixed upon was a freehold that would rent for forty shillings—that old forty-shilling freehold which for three centuries and a half had been the standing qualification for county voters in old England. In a country so wholly given up to agriculture a real-estate qualification excluded few men. In the southern colonies, it was more usual to specify a number of acres, generally fifty. The Virginian law required fifty acres of unoccupied land, or a lot of twenty-five acres with a house upon it, or a town-lot with a house upon it. But what constituted a house? If anyone thinks that our ancestors were innocent of election dodges, he may be interested in the record of one old Virginian election, that of 1762. It appears from the journals of the House of Burgesses that William Skinner had half a lot in Elizabeth City County. On the Saturday before the election he bought a small tight-framed house, ten feet by eight, and had it moved onto the land, with the acknowledged design of thereby qualifying himself to vote, and was to pay for it later. The House allowed his vote. Thomas Payne, being owner of part of a lot, says the testimony in the journal, "purchased of one Mary Almond, for the value of 10s. a small House, about 4 and a Half Feet Pitch, 4 or 5 Feet long, and 2 or 2 and a Half Feet wide, floored or laid with Plank in the Midst of its Height, to put Milkpans, or such Things, on, and that he had the same removed in a Cart, with one Horse, with the Assistance of 7 or 8 Men, and placed on his said Lot, on purpose (as he acknowledges) to qualify himself to vote at that Election." Apparently this was going a little *too* far, and the House ruled his vote out. It then passed a law requiring that the house which was to qualify the voter must be at least twelve feet square, which certainly seems moderate enough.

The Revolution greatly altered these old colonial laws respecting the franchise. Four states, it is true, made no change in their rules, but in all the rest the freehold system was broken down. In New York the value of the freehold required was reduced, and persons who merely rented land or houses were put on a par with those who owned them. In most states, any tax-payer was now allowed to vote, whether he paid taxes on real or on personal estate. In others the amount of money required was lowered. And so it came to pass, by what was primarily a political change, but one that carried the seeds of social changes, that "We the people of the

United States" who gave consent to the establishing of the Constitution was a much larger and more democratic body than "We the people of the United States" who acquiesced in the Declaration of Independence, though universal suffrage was yet a long way off.

It has been indicated already with what extensive confiscations of land the course of the Revolution had been marked. Great areas thus fell into the hands of the state governments, and most of them also possessed considerable tracts of wild lands of their own. The use made of such possessions was often such as to promote the advance of agricultural democracy. It is well known that the states were often at their wits' ends for money with which to pay their troops. In such straits an obvious resource in the case of states having a large amount of wild lands was to assign portions of them to their soldiers in lieu of pay. This was done to a very large extent, and the result was that, upon the close of the war, there set in an era of unexampled speculation in American wild lands. Soldiers sold their assignments, and the states made large sales directly, in order to pay their debts. Hence the speculation. The Duke of LaRochefoucauld-Liancourt, an émigré French nobleman who travelled extensively in the United States soon after the Revolution, tells of land near Lancaster, Pennsylvania, bought for $25 an acre, for which $100 was refused five years later. In another passage he speaks of a thousand acres near Canandaigua, New York, bought three years before at a shilling an acre, of which a half had since been sold off at prices ranging from a dollar to three dollars, and even, in some cases, twenty-five dollars. An example of one of the large sales will show, however, how low the prices would sometimes run at the great auctions, especially in the case of lands not situated near any navigable river and hence, under the conditions of transportation then prevailing, not near a market. I choose the example from the narrative of his travels printed by Henry Wansey, a Wiltshire clothier. "Monday. I attended a sale (by auction at the Tontine Coffee House) of some military lands," that is, lands given to the soldiers, "situated in the north part of New York State. Twenty-five acres in the township of Cato," he continues, "were sold at two shillings and eightpence currency" (that is, New York shillings) "per acre; . . . five hundred in Pompey at five shillings and one penny; nine hundred in Tully and Hannibal at three and eightpence; fourteen hundred in Hector and Dryden, at three and eightpence." It will be seen that the classical names which in lavish profusion decorate the map of Cortland and Onondaga counties were already there in 1789—Pompey and Tully, and Fabius and Manlius, and Cincinnatus and Marathon. It has been usual to bestow the credit or discredit of this nomenclature upon General Simeon DeWitt, the surveyor-general of the state. But the late Professor Moses Coit Tyler deemed he had proof that the dreadful deed was done by an office-boy fresh from the study of Lemprière's *Classical Dictionary*, and that the good general must be acquitted of all blame in the matter but that of leaving the selection of names to the unchastened imagination of an office-boy. However this may be, the lands sold none the less readily, 5,500,000 acres being sold by New York in a single year; and in the end, whatever allowance may be made for speculation, passed ultimately, for the most part, into the hands of small holders.

If the states, impoverished by the war and burdened with debt, found so valuable a resource through sales of state lands, we may well believe that they valued every bit of territory to which they could lay claim. Hence arose a multitude of boundary disputes, opening into several amusing but unedifying quarrels, and fostering discord between states which at that time were none too well disposed toward mutual agreement. Massachusetts found opportunity for quarrel on its western boundary with New York. Pennsylvania and Virginia differed as to the region where Pennsylvania now touches West Virginia. Virginia and North Carolina differed as to their boundary line. South Carolina and Georgia quarrelled about their boundaries at the upper part of the Savannah River, New York and New Hampshire about Vermont, Connecticut and Pennsylvania about the Wyoming country. Far more important than all these disputes was that which raged over the control of the western lands. The political history of this momentous conflict, and of its happy settlement by cessions to the Confederation, is in all the books; but the social consequences of that settlement were surely greater than any others that have been touched upon in this lecture.

In the old states, population moved more and more largely into the uplands in the western part of the state—an intermediate stage toward the trans-Allegheny migration. We may easily imagine that, on the average in the general course of the great westward movement, the typical family stayed a generation or two in that region of broken or mountainous country, a hundred or two hundred miles broad, that intervenes between the plains of the tidewater region and the levels of the Ohio and Mississippi valleys. It does not seem to me fantastic to imagine that that period of sojourn of families in the broken uplands did much to fasten the regime of small landholding on the United States. Ohio and Indiana and Kentucky were perhaps as capable physically of organization into great estates as Virginia or Carolina, but by the time the swarms of settlers debouched upon those great western plains the habit of the small farm was in the main already fixed, and the United States was to be a land of "peasant proprietors."

By the year 1789 the regions west of the mountains sustained already a considerable population. One of the most noteworthy features of American social history in the period immediately succeeding the Revolution is the prodigiously rapid migration of settlers into the new West. The movement had not waited for the Revolution to reach its slow conclusion. But in 1783, when the news of peace came to America, the stream of westward migration assumed proportions unknown before. Kentucky was erected into a district, with regular courts. Trade by way of the Ohio began. Schools were started. To the meeting-houses already built by the Baptists and Dutch Reformed was added a log church for the Presbyterians. A race-track was laid out; and Kentucky entered upon the second stage of her existence. The settlements in what is now Tennessee prospered similarly. In 1783 there were probably twenty-five thousand inhabitants in the settlements west of the Alleghenies. The number increased more rapidly in Kentucky than elsewhere. Virginia gave lands in that region to the soldiers of her disbanded forces in commutation of their claims for pay and bounty, and thus it came about that Kentucky contained in after years

an unusually large number of men who had been soldiers of
the Revolution—sturdy progenitors for an infant state. Since
the war had impoverished many of the planters of the tidewater regions of Virginia and neighboring states, many of
these now sought to repair their fortunes by a new venture,
and migrated beyond the mountains with what property they
had, to begin life anew on virgin soil. Thousands of migrants
poured into Kentucky in the long caravans that made their
difficult way over the mountains by the Wilderness Road.
Even larger numbers floated down the Ohio to the shores of
Kentucky or the newer acquisitions on the northern bank of
the river, the Illinois country, now more commonly called
the Northwest Territory. An eye-witness, writing from Kentucky in December 1785, states that, in the thirty-nine days
preceding, thirty-nine boats, with an average of ten persons
upon each, had passed down the Ohio River to the Falls. The
stream of migration increased each year. In the last half of
the year 1787 a hundred and forty-six boats passed by Fort
Harmar, conveying 3,196 persons, 1,371 horses, 165 wagons,
and cattle and sheep in proportion. In the year ending in
November 1788, a letter from that fort assures us, 967 boats
had passed down, carrying 18,370 persons, with 7,986 horses,
and with wagons and cattle and sheep. The population of
Kentucky, which in 1785 was estimated at from twenty to
thirty thousand, is stated in the census of 1790 to have been
74,000, while 37,000 more dwelt in the settlements to the
southward of Kentucky, and a few thousands in the Northwest Territory, where systematic colonization had just been
begun by the Ohio Company. With each succeeding census
the number rose with wonderful rapidity.

The movement of westward expansion which thus began is one of the most familiar facts of American history. But perhaps we do not always remember how peculiar it is, nor take notice of all its consequences. Is there any other great country whose center of population moves over the country many miles each decade, as does ours, which in a hundred and thirty years moved westward from the Chesapeake to Illinois? But what are the social results? A nation's center of population is, in a way, its center of gravity. A shifting center of gravity forces a nation into a perpetual readjustment of its life. That which was the center of the merchant's particular branch of business ten years ago is no longer its center now; the farmer, the commercial traveller, the engineer, the speculator, must learn anew, every ten years, the social geography of his country. Restless change, unceasing adaptation to new conditions, will be the characteristic of such a nation. Its members will be distinguished from those of other nations by a superior versatility, a quickness of adaptation, a readiness toward new undertakings and an openness to new ideas, such as can be bred only by past habits of perpetual readjustment and renovation.

Not less noteworthy was the influence of the western region in promoting that growth of political and social democracy which was one of the most precious legacies of the Revolutionary period. The dweller upon the broad prairies, though individual and sometimes intractable, was likely to be expansive and genial. His wide horizon was hostile to narrow views. The influx into any given area of men of all sorts and from all parts of the world tended to break up the distinctions which in more settled societies distinguished man from man. And so a hearty belief in human equality was likely to be a part of the generous creed of the West. Moreover, the very conditions of life, the intense struggle for existence which every individual had usually to go through, tended of themselves to equalize men and to draw them together in the bonds of mutual sympathy. The process, therefore, which had marked the Atlantic settlements in comparison with the countries of Europe, was likely to mark the West even more than the East, and to push forward still more the development of American democracy.

III

Industry and Commerce

Probably the World War has cured us all of the habit of supposing that a war absorbs completely the energies of a nation. So great is the stress and excitement which wars have produced, that it has been easy to imagine that, in past history, everyone has been fully occupied with them; but even in this recent instance, when war affected a greater percentage of each nation than usual, this was far from being the case. It never happens in a civilized country that even half the men of military age are in the army when the country is engaged in war. In our Civil War, the number of men between eighteen and sixty in the Union states was about five million and a half when the war broke out, but the largest number of troops in the army at any one time, including regulars, militia, and volunteers, was never much above one million, less than one-fifth. In the Confederate states, whose energies were more completely absorbed in the struggle, the army, at its largest extent, included a number equal to nearly a third of the white male population between the ages mentioned. It is plain then that, however intensely a nation may be interested in a war, the larger number of its citizens remain nevertheless occupied in other than military pursuits. They labor on the farm, in mines and factories and workshops, in their wonted vocations, in order to support themselves and to produce the wealth necessary for the maintenance of warfare. Especially is this true in a long and dragging war. Modern warfare costs so much that it is expedient that quick work be made of it, and therefore that as many men as possible be diverted from their ordinary industrial employments and put into the field or into munition-making. The industrial recuperation of the country is a matter to which they can give their attention later. But in previous centuries wars went more slowly, and it was necessary that many men should remain at their homes and continue the ordinary work of industrial production. King Alfred, it will be remembered, divided his West-Saxon army into two equal divisions, that one might remain in the field while the other attended to the labors of their rude agriculture.

At the time when the Revolutionary war broke out, the population of the thirteen colonies amounted to about two and a half million men, women, and children. The number of men of fighting age, say from eighteen to sixty, would then be something like seven hundred thousand. A much smaller proportion of them was in the fighting force of General Washington than that which the United States of 1865 yielded to the army of General Grant. In 1776, when the army was at its largest, it numbered, including both Continentals and state militia, not quite ninety thousand men, about one-eighth of the men of fighting age. In the years 1779 and 1780 it was but half as large, not more than a sixteenth part of the male inhabitants of military age. And, of the seven years of the war, more were like 1779 and 1780 than like 1776.

The thought need only be suggested, how widespread an apathy is evidenced by these figures, even after we have made allowance for the thousands of brave sailors who were fighting the battles of the Revolution in naval vessels and privateers. The figures are mentioned rather to show that, ardently as many thousands were engaged in the actual work of fighting, for most men in the thirteen American states industrial life went on during these seven years, not without disturbance, to be sure, but without cessation in its development. It may be profitable to turn aside from the stirring records of military achievement, to see what was being done in agriculture, in manufactures, and in commerce during the same period, and how far and in what ways, if at all, their development was affected by the war and the political revolution.

It was remarked in the preceding lecture that vastly the greater number of the people of the American colonies were occupied with agriculture. It will therefore be proper to begin with this industry though it was affected less by the Revolution than some other classes of occupation. One very important series of effects has been touched upon in the last lecture, the freeing of the soil from all connection with the feudal land-law, the breaking-up of large estates, the universal extension, in the North at least, of that system of small or moderate farms, cultivated by the owner's own hands, which so long remained the characteristic mark of the agricultural system of America.

Throughout the colonial period, American agriculture was still in a stage of experimentation, as was natural in a new country to which farmers came from an old country. Farmers had tested the suitableness of the American soil and climate to the agricultural products of Europe so thoroughly that hardly a single important species of domestic animal and hardly a single important species of cultivated plant originating in Europe, has, it is said, been introduced since the Revolutionary War. But American agriculture had been careless and wasteful. Land was so cheap and labor so much scarcer than in Europe that it did not pay to apply to American soil the careful intensive cultivation of England and France. The result was that, in the times just preceding the Revolution, colonial agriculture was in a poor condition. The fields had been worn out by hasty methods, and better methods were not learned because, with all the experimenting that had gone on, the results of experience were not diffused among farmers, for lack of agricultural societies and periodicals.

Meanwhile, during the middle portion of the eighteenth century, the agriculture of England and France had been undergoing improvements so great as almost to constitute a revolution in methods. But little of this revival found its way to America, and that mainly through the efforts of one man, and he a clergyman. The Rev. Jared Eliot, grandson of the apostle John Eliot, was for nearly half a century pastor of the church at Killingworth, Connecticut. He was a member of the Royal Society in London, and as a physician in difficult cases had so great repute that he was even called to Newport and Boston for such purposes. This man, after travels in Europe extending even as far as Russia, brought home the knowledge of good methods of agriculture, wrote and published essays, tried experiments on his Connecticut farm, introduced clover-sowing for the recuperation of worn-out fields, and was in many ways useful in his day and generation. But in general the better modes of cultivation which Europe had lately been learning were but little known in the American colonies when the war began. In particular, the domestic animals of America were, on account of the inferiority of the native American grasses, much smaller and poorer than those of Europe. Indeed, the opinion prevailed in Europe that all animated nature degenerated on the western continent, and the chief of naturalists, Buffon, set forth this view in his writings, until Jefferson, to confute him, sent to America for the skeleton of an elk.

But the Revolution brought American farmers into more intimate association with Europeans, and especially with Frenchmen, and thus gave them a chance to learn more of the recent agricultural improvements. Their minds were widened by the war. Best of all, the organizing habit which was bred in the American mind by this period of political and social reorganization gave an impetus to the much-needed formation of agricultural societies. These had been in Europe the most important means of disseminating information regarding improved methods or the results of experiment, and of awakening the minds of farmers. In Scotland the "Society of Improvers in the Knowledge of Agriculture" had been formed in 1723, and others had followed during the next decades. Agriculture, which had been practically stationary from the times of the Roman Empire, began to awaken from its long sleep. Now, as soon as the Revolution was over, societies of similar purpose began to be formed in America. The first such in the United States was the "Society for the Promotion of Agriculture" founded at Charleston, South Carolina, in August 1785. The Philadelphia society of the same name was founded later in the same year, that of New York in 1791, those of Massachusetts and Connecticut in 1792.

These societies began a most valuable work of experiment, comparison, and diffusion of information. The cast-iron plough began to be introduced. The cradle began to supplant the sickle. Efforts were made to improve livestock, in spite of the severe laws which forbade under heavy penalties the exportation of south-downs from England or merinos from Spain. And farming, as it grew more skilful, grew more profitable. The English economist, Dr. Thomas Cooper, in his book of information for persons intending to emigrate to the United States, advises the man of middling fortune to become a farmer there. (He adds, among his items of minor advice, that the intending emigrant had better take flower-seeds with him, since the Americans care so much more for utility than for ornament that flower-seeds are hard to procure in the States.)

American manufactures were much more directly and conspicuously affected by the Revolution than American agriculture. In the first place, the Revolution did away at once with all those annoying restrictions with which the English Parliament had endeavored to burden colonial manufactures. In the long list of American grievances against the British government, not the least had been the series of petty enactments by which it had been sought to confine the colonies to the production of raw materials, while England monopolized the manufacturing industries of both countries. So early as 1699 the woollen manufactures of New England had become large enough to attract the attention of old England. An act was passed in that year to prevent, under heavy penalties, the export from the colonies, or from colony to colony, of any "Wool, Woolfells, Shortlings, Morlings, Wool Flocks, Worsted, Bay or Woollen Yarn, Cloath, Serge, Bays, Kerseys, Says, Frizes, Druggets, Cloath Serges, Shalloons or any other Drapery, Stuffs or Woollen Manufactures whatsoever." In 1719 the House of Commons resolved "that the erection of manufactories in the colonies tends to lessen their dependence on Great Britain." The plentiful supply of beaver in the colonies led to a considerable manufacture of hats. In 1732 an act of Parliament was passed which forbade the exportation of hats from the colonies, and prohibited any hatter from taking more than two apprentices. The iron manufacture grew. England welcomed the increased supply of pig and bar iron, but wished absolutely to engross to herself all further manufactures. In 1750 Parliament prohibited the erection of any rolling-, slitting-, or plating-mill, and all manufacture of steel. In this, as in so many other ways, the Revolution enfranchised America. American manufactures might henceforth be developed solely in accordance with American interests.

Again, the non-importation agreements and the war which speedily ensued cut off at once nearly all of the stream of goods hitherto imported from England. The colonists were thrown back upon their own resources. For eight years they were obliged, for the most part, either to get along without these goods, which in some cases was very difficult, or to provide them for themselves. American ingenuity, already developed by the various needs of a pioneer civilization, was set to work to devise, as well as it could, the means of supplying its own wants independently of England or Europe.

Even before the passage of the Stamp Act such results were foreshadowed. A letter from a Virginian to a correspondent in Bristol, England, written in the autumn of 1764, says: "The Acts of Parliament have made such impressions on the minds of the northward people and the men-of-war so strictly enforce them, that there is an entire stagnation of trade. Nothing do they talk of but their own manufactures. The downfall of England and the rise of America is sung by the common ballad-singers about the streets, as if in a little time we should supply ourselves with most of the necessaries we used before to take from England."

At New York there was immediately formed a "Society for the Promotion of Arts, Agriculture, and Economy." Great efforts were made to foster the manufacture of linens and woollens. Large numbers of people agreed to abstain from the use of mourning at funerals, such as black cloth, scarfs, gloves, and rings, not of domestic manufacture, and a useful simplification of funerals resulted. To keep up the supply of material for woollen manufactures, most of the inhabitants agreed not to eat any lamb or mutton, and not to deal with any butcher who should kill any lambs.

This movement was so extensive as to produce a genuine effect of alarm among the merchants in Great Britain. When Townshend, in 1767, proposed his duties on paper, glass, painters' colors, and tea, the enthusiasm for domestic manufactures revived. Resolutions were made to abstain from the use of "loaf sugar, . . . coaches and carriages of all sorts, imported hats and clothing, . . . gold, silver, and thread lace, gold and silver buttons," plate, diamonds, clocks, watches, jewelry, muffs, furs, millinery, starch, women's and children's stays, velvet, gauze, silks, and many other articles more difficult to do without. The spinning-wheel came into renewed use in every household, and homespun was worn by the wealthiest. Spinning matches at neighbors' houses became a common occurrence, and an excellent outlet for patriotic ardor. Imports from England into the northern colonies went down in 1769 to not much more than a third of what they were in 1768. Hence the repeal of all the taxes save that on tea. At Harvard Commencement, in 1770, the graduating class appeared in black cloth entirely of American manufacture.

The Virginia Convention of August 1774 resolved that attention should be turned "from the cultivation of tobacco to the cultivation of such articles as may form a basis for domestic manufactures, which we will endeavor to encourage throughout this Colony to the utmost of our abilities." The first Continental Congress recommended to all the colonies the encouragement of manufactures. The colonies offered bounties and prizes, and encouraged the formation of societies of arts. In 1775 the "United Company of Philadelphia for promoting American Manufactures" was formed, to organize on a large scale the making of American woollen, linen, and cotton cloth. It continued, with varying fortunes, and supplied a part of the cloth for the Revolutionary army. A great part of the privations which that army suffered arose from the undeveloped state of the manufacturing industries of the country. Woollen materials were hardly to be had for love or money, and the soldiers often shivered through a campaign in clothing chiefly consisting of linen. At Baltimore, we are told, General Lafayette was invited to a ball. He went, but did not dance. Instead, he addressed the ladies: "You are very handsome, you dance very prettily, your ball is very fine—but my soldiers have no shirts." They ran home and went to work, and in a few days the product of their energy and industry was placed at the service of the marquis.

The intense demand for woollen goods reacted upon the manufacture of machinery for making them. Great attention was given in several states to the devising of new processes for making wool-cards. Indeed, the Revolution brought out in strong relief the inventiveness of the American, a trait for which he is now so famous, and which a century and a half of life in a new country had powerfully developed in private, but which now came forward prominently into public notice. Patents and bounties began to be granted by governments, and there began to be famous inventors, like Oliver Evans and Amos Whittemore, in the place of the inglorious genius, farmer or farm-hand, who could make anything with a jack-knife, but whose fame did not extend beyond his village.

It was natural that in the development of certain classes of manufacture the Revolution should have a peculiar importance. There were arms and munitions of war to be provided, for instance. Great Britain in 1774 forbade the exportation of fire-arms, gun-powder, and other military stores. Some manufacture of them had already begun in the colonies. But now Congress and the state Committees of Safety took hold of the matter as a thing of vital importance in the struggle. For the making of gunpowder, saltpeter was collected from old cellars and stables. As for arms, though the Americans had not made them in great numbers, they had become very skilful in the art, as was natural in a nation so full of hunters. Governor Richard Penn, in his examination before the House of Lords just as the war was beginning, stated, in reply to the inquiries of the Duke of Richmond, that the casting of iron and brass cannon at Philadelphia had been carried to great perfection, and that the workmanship and finish of the small arms was all that could be desired. Rifles were made in the colonies at that time which were thought as good as any that were imported. Gunsmiths were numerous. But in this, as in other trades, there was little organization. Each gunsmith worked for himself, or perhaps had two or three men to help him, so that the committees of Congress had to make their contracts for small quantities, and place them here and there with individuals, and, after all, to get most of their arms from Europe.

In 1778 the government armory at Springfield was established, where the works would be remote from the incursions of the enemy. For a similar reason, much gun-making was carried on in Maryland. To stimulate the manufacture of such things, Congress called upon the states to exempt from taxation all who were engaged in them. That they were sometimes at the greatest straits for material, may well be imagined, when all the ordinary channels of trade were closed or perverted. We hear of one foundry idle for a long time from sheer want of copper. A few days before the battle of Brandywine, messengers were sent to the mills of the Dunkers or German "Brethren" at Ephrata for a supply of paper for cartridges. The mill's products happened to be exhausted, so far as clean paper was concerned. But the fraternity also did a printing business, and had on hand an edition of Fox's *Book of Martyrs,* in sheets, then ready for the bindery. They generously placed this mass of printed paper at the service of their country, and in the ensuing battle the good old martyrologist, in the form of cartridges, went up in smoke and flames for the good cause, like the martyrs of whom he wrote.

Paper-mills increased enormously during the Revolutionary period. One important reason for this was the great increase of newspapers. There were thirty-seven in 1776. In 1789 there were probably over a hundred. The addiction of the American to this sort of reading was already remarkable. "All these people," says the Duke of LaRochefoucauld of the people of the house at which he was stopping in Marlborough, Massachusetts, "busy themselves much with politics, and from the landlord down to the housemaid they all read two newspapers a day."

It will perhaps hardly be imagined that, of the manufactures which the Revolution directly affected, one of those most highly stimulated was that of salt. Before the Revolution, the saline deposits of central New York and of the remoter interior had not yet been reached, and salt was almost altogether procured from abroad. It was an article of prime importance to the Americans, partly because of the great amounts used in the fisheries, partly because it was much given to cattle, and largely also because our fathers made so enormous use of salted provisions and exported so many barrels of them. The chief supply of salt had been obtained by the ships which went out with lumber, fish and other provisions, and tobacco. When they came back, they often brought coarse salt as ballast, from the ports of southern Europe, the Canary or Madeira or West Indian Islands.

The interruption of this trade produced a distressing scarcity of salt. It rose to six dollars a bushel. Many attempts were made, all along the shore of the Atlantic, to procure salt by boiling sea-water in kettles. Finally, an enterprising sailor residing upon Cape Cod conceived the idea of making salt more economically, after the manner followed in the Mediterranean, by evaporation by the sun's heat acting on sea-water in large and shallow vats. Soon many such went into operation, and the wind-mills by which the salt water was pumped up became a noteworthy feature of the not-too-varied scenery of the Cape. This particular manufacture, being of necessity carried on in positions near the sea, was more than ordinarily exposed to the destructive attacks of the British. But it developed in the United States a considerable industry.

On the other hand, the war destroyed for the time that which had been before the war the chief of American manufactures for exportation, namely, shipbuilding. Writers in that time and since have been fond of declaiming against the oppressiveness of the Navigation Acts. Their burden was in many ways difficult to bear—or would have been had they not been so systematically and successfully evaded by the enterprising colonists. But it is certain that they fostered American shipbuilding in the highest degree. In the years 1769, 1770, and 1771, nearly four hundred vessels a year, large and small, were built in the colonies. When the war broke out, 400,000 tons of colonial-built shipping were employed in the general commerce of Great Britain. The severing of the political connection with England deprived American shipwrights of this advantage, and for a time their trade languished, but after the peace it recovered with surprising swiftness.

It is not possible to dwell upon all the varieties of manufacture which the Revolution called into existence or stimulated in America, though it would be pleasant to speak of the development of the piano-forte, whose prodigious frequency in all subsequent times might easily deceive unwary travellers into the belief that we were a musical people. The leading manufactures when the war ended, suffice it to say, were, beside those that have been mentioned, those from iron and leather, and that of glass. Europeans believed that, when the artificial stimulus produced by the war was withdrawn, many of these would not continue to succeed. Dr. Cooper, an intelligent and fair-minded man, thought it would be a long time before manufactures of woollen, linen, and cotton goods, or of pottery, would succeed. Wages were too high. "I have no doubt, however," he says, "of the success of a glass manufacture, a gunpowder manufacture, of a paper maker, a paper stainer, a letter founder, a manufactory of all the heavy kinds of iron-work, such as castings from the ore, pig iron, bar iron, rolling mills, slitting mills, and the making of nails." Of most of these there were already examples in the country by the year 1789. To illustrate the increase of mills of various sorts, the Duke of LaRochefoucauld says that, ten years after the Revolution, Brandywine Creek, in the seven or eight miles of its short course through Delaware, turned about sixty mills.

But it should be understood that but a small part of the manufacturing enterprise which the Revolution evoked expended itself in manufacturing establishments. The bulk of American manufacturing was after all domestic. In most parts of the country by far the greatest part of the clothing was made in the household. When Tench Coxe investigated this subject, a few years later, he said that typical neighborhoods of twenty families rich and poor, in Virginia, showed in one case domestic manufactures of the value of $1670 in one year, in the other of $1791. For another evidence of their extent, we know that there were forty-one fulling-mills in New Jersey at a time when there were in that state no established manufactories of cloth, none, that is, other than the domestic; also, that one shop in Philadelphia, a few years after the Revolution, sold in one year fifteen hundred sets of spinning-wheel irons.

This domestic mode was often employed in trades to which we should hardly think of its being applicable now. Take for instance, the manufacture of nails. It was one of those branches in which the country earliest became independent of British supplies, and one of those in which the effects of the war were first felt among British manufacturers—at least so said Lord Dudley in the House of Peers in 1776. Yet it was in very large part, if not chiefly, a domestic manufacture. In one of the first debates in the House of Representatives, Fisher Ames of Massachusetts said: "This manufacture, with very little encouragement, has grown up very remarkably. It has become common for the country people in Massachusetts to erect small forges in their chimney corners, and in winter, and on evenings when little other work can be done, great quantities of nails are made, even by children. These people take the rod-iron of the merchant and return him the nails, and in consequence of this easy mode of barter, the manufacture is prodigiously great." This bit may serve to show us that, if it seems a long distance from these humble beginnings to the vast industrial development of today, nevertheless the industry and grit were already present which were in time to make this the greatest manufacturing country of the world.

If we turn now to the consideration of internal trade, it is easy to see that here the war could do little but harm to the industrial life of the country. A comparatively poor country, being compelled to manage an expensive war, of necessity had recourse to large issues of paper money. Millions upon millions were sent forth. Each one of the thirteen states issued notes which competed for circulation with those of the Continental Congress. In December 1778, the Continental bills, then considerably exceeding a hundred millions in amount, had depreciated until they were worth only a twentieth part of their face value. Yet Congress maintained the certainty of their redemption, and resolved "that any contrary report was false, and derogatory to its honor." In August 1779, a paper dollar was worth only three or four cents in silver. In December it was worth less than two and a half cents. "A wagon-load of money," it was said, "would scarcely purchase a wagon-load of provisions." In April 1781, Congress proposed an exchange of the old bills for new, at the rate of forty dollars for one, and the measure was received with favor, though it wiped out at one stroke thirty-nine fortieths of such debt as was represented by the paper money. A Philadelphia wag made a blanket for his dog out of the Continental paper, and paraded him upon the street in that array.

Under such circumstances it was hardly to be expected that trade should flourish, even in regions which did not not feel heavily the pressure of war and were not in danger from incursions or depredations of the enemy. Prices went up and up. Conventions of counties, and finally conventions at which several states were represented, met, for instance at Providence, at Springfield, at Hartford, and at Yorktown, and attempted to bolster up the failing credit of the paper money by laws declaring that the prices of commodities should not rise above certain figures enumerated upon their lists. Nevertheless prices rose. Economic laws were stronger than those of state legislatures, however resolute and patriotic. In 1781 we find quotations of shoes at twenty pounds a pair, milk at fifteen shillings a quart, potatoes at ninety shillings a bushel, rum at forty-five shillings a quart, corn at forty dollars a bushel, a cow at $1200.

The depreciation, of course, bore hardest upon men who lived upon salaries, or in other ways had fixed incomes. Dr. Ezra Ripley, who was settled over the parish of Concord, Massachusetts, in 1788, gives a vivid account of his trials in his *Half-Century Discourse* preached in 1828. He says: "With all his exertions in various ways, as teaching scholars, manual labor, etc., your pastor could not have waded through, had it not been for a particular event in Providence, and the long credit given him by one benevolent trader (Deacon John White) in town." For those whose deacons were not benevolent, as no doubt sometimes happened, there must have been many privations while the currency was in this disordered condition.

It should be remembered, also, how lacking in the colonies were the most ordinary facilities for the transaction of large business. Transportation was in an almost primitive condition. It casts a flash of light upon the provinciality of American life at the time of the Declaration of Independence, to reflect that at that time there was not a single bank in the whole country. The first organized bank in the United States, the Bank of North America, had its origin in a meeting of citizens of Philadelphia, in June 1780, to devise means of furnishing supplies to the army, then in a state of great destitution. It was then resolved to open a "security subscription to the amount of £300,000, Pennsylvania currency, real money." Robert Morris subscribed ten thousand pounds to this fund, and Tom Paine five hundred dollars. Morris made the plan for the Bank of North America, which was chartered by Congress on the last day of the year 1781. The charter permitted a capital of ten million dollars, but individuals paid in only $85,000, and the government, which subscribed $250,000, paid in only $50,000. The bank began its career with $300,000. Besides this pioneer bank, which is still in existence, only two others had come into operation in 1789, the Massachusetts Bank in Boston, and the Bank of New York.

One branch of American industrial life made great gains because of the war, to which we have not yet alluded, and that is maritime commerce. Under all the restrictions imposed by the Navigation Acts, American commerce had been constantly growing, and there were even merchant princes in some of the greater ports, or traders so esteemed in that day. The war interrupted commerce greatly, of course. It could not fail to do so, in view of the prodigious navy of Great Britain.

Nevertheless it furnished the maritime development of the nation, and that in two ways, first by stimulating privateering adventure, and secondly by removing legal restrictions and opening a free course to American shipping into all parts of the world save those under British control. Privateering was of course a mode of warfare, but the impulse that led men into it was largely commercial, or at least that same love of gain which also inspired commerce.

The Americans were old hands at privateering. In the War of the Spanish Succession, in the Spanish war of 1739, the French war of 1744, and especially in the French and Indian War, the business had attained prodigious proportions. In 1745, Captain Simeon Potter, of Bristol, Rhode Island, sailing in the *Prince Charles of Lorraine,* had ravaged fifteen hundred miles of territory on the Spanish Main. In one cruise, in 1759 and 1760, Abraham Whipple of Rhode Island captured twenty-three prizes, valued at a million dollars. Now when the Revolution broke out the memory of these exploits and receipts was still fresh, and New England had many skilful seamen idle because of the serious interruption to the fisheries which had been caused by the presence of the British warships off the coast. Here was all the material for a great development of privateering enterprise.

Sometimes it is difficult to distinguish, in the maritime history of the Revolution, what was naval endeavor, carried on in government vessels, which was war, from that which was carried on in private vessels, which was half war, half business. But it seems clear that the privateering successes of the Revolution quite overshadowed those obtained by the vessels of the federal and state governments, and that they made more impression upon the enemy. Service on a privateer was more attractive to bold sailors, for it offered prospects of greater gains. So great were the profits that New England shipping interests, it is said, were never more prosperous than in the last years of the war. In 1781 Salem alone had fifty-nine vessels, carrying four thousand men. In the year preceding, the Admiralty Court of the Essex district of Massachusetts had condemned 818 prizes. In the single month of May 1779 eighteen prizes were brought into New London. In the course of the whole war more than five hundred privateers were commissioned by the various states, and probably as many as ninety thousand Americans were, first and last, engaged in these voyages, a number of men almost as great as served in the army, and greater than that of the army in any single year save one. Two-thirds of these men were from Massachusetts, the rest from the other New England states and from the Delaware river.

A good notion of the importance of the privateers' exploits may be gained from the fact that in 1776 insurance on cargoes going from the West Indies to England rose to twenty-eight per cent of the value of the ship and goods. Special types of vessels were developed for these purposes, and American designs in shipbuilding permanently benefited. "Thousands of schemes of privateering," wrote John Adams, "are afloat in American imaginations." At the end of that year, 1776, no less than two hundred and fifty West Indiamen had been captured, and the injury already done to the West India trade was estimated in England at £1,800,000. Robert Morris is said to have raised his fortune to between £300,000 and £400,000 by such ventures. Abraham Whipple, in the *Providence*, once fell in with a large convoy of English merchantmen bound from the West Indies to England. He disguised his vessel, or concealed her character, so that he boldly entered the fleet as one of their number. After dark on each of ten successive nights he boarded and captured some vessel from the convoy. Upon each of these he put a small prize crew and sent it away secretly to Boston. Eight of them reached that port, and their cargoes sold for more than a million dollars. Beside exploits in the nearer waters, the privateers sought their gain in remoter seas. Even the waters around Britain were not safe from them, and the privateer *General Mifflin* hovered around the North Cape and took seven or eight English vessels on their way to Archangel.

All this would have various effects upon the development of regular commerce. It would immensely stimulate boldness and enterprise on the part of captains and sailors. If when peace was made they could bring themselves down from these sublime heights of romantic adventure to the sober level of peaceful trade at all, it must be trade with a spice of adventure in it at least.

One of the least happy avenues through which this spirit of venture found expression was the revival of the African slave trade. In years just before the outbreak of hostilities that traffic was flourishing. During the war importations into the Continental colonies ceased almost entirely. The natural effect in the West Indies was a glut of the market. Peace was promptly followed by a great revival of the trade. Not only had the planters been deprived during seven years of the opportunity for their customary buying, but they had also lost many of their negroes by the depredations of the invading army. So rapid was the increase in importations into South Carolina that by 1785 that state was once more debating the wisdom of curtailing the traffic, at least for a time. During the course of the debate it was stated that 7000 negroes had been imported into Charleston since the peace. The assembly passed a law forbidding importations, effective in 1787. In Rhode Island a law was passed forbidding any citizen of the state to take part in the trade. Thereafter any participation in it by Rhode Islanders was illicit and furtive.

In forms more respectable a pronounced taste for longer voyages, for trade with remoter regions, is found among seamen when the war ended. In 1783 men began to talk in Salem of the China trade. The Orient had for them something of the same charm which it had exercised upon the minds of Prince Henry the Navigator and Vasco da Gama. If the traders themselves had no gift of any but prosaic expression, who shall say, nevertheless, that there was not a poetic element in this looking toward a wider horizon for the expansive influence of the young republic?

At all events the new trade went on. In 1784 Captain John Green, in the *Empress,* sailed direct from New York to Canton. The *Grand Turk,* Captain West, made a voyage that year to the Cape of Good Hope, and in 1785 to the Isle of France and Canton. So rapidly was the trade pushed that in 1789, only four years later, a British observer reports that, of eighty-six ships in the harbor of Canton, fifteen were American. Brissot says that in that same year forty-four vessels sailed out of Boston alone for the Northwest Coast, the East Indies, and China. Many of these ships were in the command of boys under twenty-one.

The incentive to the trade was the enormous profits which might be made by these direct voyages to regions with which the colonies had traded only indirectly. The usual profit on muslins and calicoes from Calcutta was a hundred per cent. The ship *Benjamin Silsbee* took less than $1,000 worth of plain glass tumblers to the Isle of France, and sold them for $12,000. Ebenezer Parsons, a younger brother of Chief Justice Parsons, sent vessels from Gloucester to the Indies, which then carried cargoes of coffee around to Smyrna, making large profits, sometimes as much as three hundred or four hundred per cent. Everyone knows the story of Lord Timothy Dexter and his cargo of warming-pans, but that was of a later time.

But beside such effects as arose from heightened boldness and enterprise, the Revolution affected American commerce in another and very substantial way. It is familiar that, among the grievances that gave rise to the Revolution, none was more insisted upon than the Navigation Acts. These purported to confine the commerce of the colonies for the benefit of the mother country. Most colonial products could be sent abroad only to English ports. It is quite true that the laws were extensively evaded; nevertheless they did operate to some extent. Therefore the Declaration of Independence brought to American commerce a release from fetters. The commerce of the world, except with England, was thrown open to the new United States. Even before independence was declared, the Continental Congress had so far relaxed the American Association as to permit the export of produce to all countries not under British rule, and free trade in all goods not of British origin. New channels of trade were thus at once opened. Shipments of tobacco and other staples were made to France, Spain, and Holland, either directly or through the West Indian possessions of those countries, which had a great demand for American lumber, fish, and salted meat. Indirectly, it proved possible to keep up a trade, though at some risk in case of discovery, with the British West Indies also. The intermediary was St. Eustatius, a little Dutch island of the Caribbean group, which had a good roadstead and was a free port. Here the goods of the revolted colonies of the mainland could be exchanged against those of the still loyal colonies of the West Indies, much to the advantage of both, for we are told that the cessation of the ordinary supplies from the mainland colonies had caused in Jamaica alone the starvation of fifteen thousand negroes. When Rodney captured St. Eustatius in 1781, sober authorities estimated the value of the capture at more than three million pounds sterling.

By all such means, American commerce began to recover from the first shocks and losses of war. In April 1777, a Boston merchant writes: "Though our money has depreciated, the internal strength of the Country is greater than when the war began; and there is hardly a town that has not more ratable polls than at that time. And though many individuals suffer, yet the farmer and the bulk of the people gain by the war; and Great Britain therefore ought not to think of ever getting a peace without allowing independence." That the people who surrounded him were not without the comforts and even the luxuries of life is evident from other passages in his letters. French silks, cambrics, etc., are called for. "I would observe," he says, "that people dress as much and as extravagantly as ever. The ladies lay out much on their heads, in flowers and white gauze; and hoop petticoats seem crawling in."

We must not deny that the war brought with it, as all wars do, great losses and great derangements of economic and industrial life. But, so far as commerce was concerned, it brought with it the brightest promise of wider and richer development in the future. Not, however, in the immediate future. For, in spite of all that has been said, one great obstacle hindered for six years after the conclusion of peace in 1783 the best development of American trade, whether domestic or foreign. Nothing is more necessary to the life of trade than a strong and firm government. Now it is notorious that the government of the United States under the Confederation was abjectly weak and uncertain. The government of the United States had no power to raise money to pay its debts, no power to give stability to the currency or stay the depreciation of its own promises to pay, no power to compel the states to keep their promises or do justice, or even to keep the peace with each other, no power to preserve them from internal discords and insurrections, no power to provide a uniform tariff law, so necessary for the successful calculations of merchants, no power to secure to foreign creditors their just dues, no power to execute its own treaties, no power to keep up a satisfactory consular service, no power even to regulate port dues and lighthouses. Taxes were resisted, and all manner of economic heresies were afloat.

Thus the newly-arisen enterprise in commerce, which the war had called into existence, found itself hampered by the weakness of the federal organization. This furnishes the explanation of the fact that, in all the efforts which statesmen were making in these years from 1783 to 1789 to erect a stronger federal government, they found their best helpers among the commercial classes. To these the necessity for a stronger government was so apparent that it did not need argument. Hence it should not surprise us that the pathway to the creation of a firmer union led through considerations of commercial regulations. The conferences about the regulation of commerce between Maryland and Virginia, held at Alexandria and at Mount Vernon in 1785, paved the way to the Annapolis Convention, which in 1786 met to consider the policy of such regulations between a larger number of the states or, if possible, the whole union. From the Annapolis Convention of 1786 sprang the Philadelphia Convention of 1787, which framed the Constitution of the United States. And as commerce helped to bring about the better union, so the firmer union helped to forward commerce. From the time of the adoption of that constitution, American shipping entered upon an era of immense prosperity, which speedily gave unbounded fame to the merchant marine of the United States.

Upon the statue of the first William Pitt which the City of London erected in his honor in the midst of that hive of industry, they placed an inscription commemorating him as that great minister who had made trade flourish by means of war. So remarkable a commendation no statesman of our Revolution could have claimed, nor have I any desire to maintain that that war was not, like nearly every other war, accompanied by great losses and injuries to our economic system. What I have tried to show is, that American industry profited by it in the end. The Civil War of sixty years ago, which so desolated and impoverished the South, nevertheless, by sweeping away an obsolete economic and social system, set free the economic life of the South, to enter upon that career of varied and boundless prosperity of which we have seen only the beginnings. The effort of this lecture has been to show in what ways the Revolution brought ultimate benefit to the agriculture, the manufactures, and the commerce of the United States of America.

IV

Thought and Feeling

The preceding lectures have concerned themselves solely with the visible or tangible effects which the American Revolution brought about in the social system of America. The imponderable effects which it may have caused in the field of public opinion or popular emotion are not so easily identified or traced. One reason for this rests upon the fundamental fact that in the order of time causes are presumed to precede effects. We cannot satisfy ourselves as to these relations of cause and effect unless we can establish our chronological sequences with some security, and in the realm of popular thought and feeling it is difficult to date most of the phenomena. It is difficult even when a country has an abundant literature, and certainly the United States of 1783 was far from literary. In the main its population was inarticulate, and the few who wrote were as likely to be expressing thoughts which they had found in European books as thoughts which originated or were current among American minds.

Again, many movements which we may trace in American thought and feeling, and which we may ascribe to the influence of the American Revolution on the principle of *post hoc, propter hoc*, may have been due to causes of worldwide range, operative in Europe quite as much as in America, with effects perceptible in countries that had had nothing to do with the American Revolution. Of the waves of thought and feeling that in past times have disturbed Europe, the most important have not failed to cross the Atlantic, though often they have arrived on these shores so transformed as not to be at once recognized. If, for instance, we compare the European revolutionary movements of 1830 and those of 1848, we perceive that they were strikingly different in character. The animating cause of the revolutions of 1830 was social discontent, that of the revolutions of 1848 was the sentiment of nationalism. Now what do we see on this side of the water? No revolutions, in either year. But in the early 'thirties we see abundant evidences of social ferment—transcendentalism and socialism, antislavery agitation and Mormonism, passionate advocacy of Graham bread and this or that medical panacea, wild financial as well as philosophical speculation, workingmen's parties, free love, and a tendency toward riots. Plainly all this constituted the American phase of the revolutionary ferment of 1830.

In 1848, on the other hand, we see in the United States no revolutions indeed, but all the symptoms of heightened nationalism—the war with Mexico, the threat of war with Great Britain, the fervor of annexationism, the proclaiming of "Manifest Destiny," the height of spread-eagle oratory—all those phenomena, in short, which led the late Professor

Dunning to give to his chapter on this period the expressive title of "The Roaring Forties."

Going further back, I do not think it fantastic to discover an American phase of that modulation of key in the intellectual life of Europe, at the end of the eighteenth century and the beginning of the nineteenth, which we call the Romantic Movement. We should hardly look for many literary manifestations of it, in a land so little literary, but we may rightly see its outcroppings in the religious movements typified in the emotional revivals which in just those years stirred so deeply the forest communities of the West.

We shall, then, in any consideration of the American Revolution as a source of change in American thought and feeling, make large allowance for the working of causes that were nowise confined to the United States, for influences that, in all countries, were in the air during the years in question. Thus, it would be pleasant to think that humane influences playing about the Revolution were the cause of the movement toward prison reform of which the serious beginning may be found in the formation in 1787 of the "Philadelphia Society for Alleviating the Miseries of Public Prisons." It is true that the Americans were, as I think they still are, somewhat more humane than most other peoples, and an English historian justly commends in particular the humanity with which they conducted the Revolutionary War. Their criminal code was far less savage than that of England, where when our Revolution opened two hundred offenses were punishable with death; in none of the American colonies did the number exceed twenty, and two states, Virginia and Pennsylvania, considerably softened their penal codes within our period. Four of the states ameliorated their laws respecting the imprisonment of poor debtors, under which half the population of a prison sometimes consisted of that class and a case is recorded where seven of them were kept in prison for debts aggregating less than seven pounds.

The Revolution may have had something to do with such legislation, for the changes of fortune incident to a wildly fluctuating currency and a period of exceptional speculation probably brought into the debtors' prisons a new class of unfortunates, embracing many persons of whom legislators had personal knowledge, bringing personal compassion. Also, the frequent passage of stay-laws during the war and in the years immediately following it may have caused a more lenient feeling toward debtors to prevail. When, however, we consider how slowly the amelioration of prisons and of the penal code and of the condition of debtors proceeded, and in how few states before the end of the century, it is more reasonable to attribute what progress was made, here as in Europe, rather to the writings of Beccaria and the labors of John Howard, or in general terms to the *Zeitgeist*, than to any supposed influence of our Revolution.

On the other hand, many immediate influences from the Revolution can be securely traced. In the first place, the mere fact of independence caused the American to think and feel differently about America. Joel Barlow's *Vision of Columbus*, or President Stiles's celebrated election sermon on *The United States elevated to Glory and Honor*, could not possibly have been written twenty years earlier. Rather oddly to modern apprehension, but naturally enough when the political circumstances of the time are considered, in many cases it is the elevation of his colony to the position of an independent or sovereign state that seems to affect the citizen's mind with pride, rather than any larger aspect of independence. An evidence of this heightening of state pride may be seen in the fact that—Virginia, Massachusetts, Jamaica, New York, and New Jersey having, to be sure, already provided themselves with good colonial histories—writers in the younger and smaller states proceeded in just these years after the Revolution to prepare excellent histories of their respective states: Belknap's *New Hampshire,* Ramsay's *South Carolina,* Williamson's *North Carolina,* Proud's *Pennsylvania,* Trumbull's *Connecticut,* and the unfinished and unpublished histories of Rhode Island and of Georgia by Theodore Foster and Edward Langworthy.

Our own generation is abundantly familiar with the legacy which war leaves behind it in the form of what is called postwar psychology. The types of its manifestation are recurrent. The profiteer, the *nouveau riche,* the *Incroyable,* the flapper, are found, under varying designations, alike in 1784 or in 1796 or in 1816 or in 1866 or in 1919. Sober Americans of 1784 lamented the spirit of speculation which war and its attendant disturbances had generated, the restlessness of the young, their disrespect for tradition and authority, the increase of crime, the frivolity and extravagance of society.

There were more specific sequelae of warfare. There was the duel, for instance. Before the French and Indian War there had been few instances of it in America. Contact with British officers in that war had shown young American officers that the duel was the hallmark of military sophistication. Contact with French officers during the Revolutionary

War fastened in the minds of young American officers, from whom it spread to many others, the belief that, if greatly displeased with the conduct of a fellow-citizen toward you, your proper course was to offer him an opportunity to kill you. This fantastic but not ignoble superstition persisted in many parts of America almost till the Civil War, and its upholders were as certain as Moltke was concerning warfare, that its abandonment would entail the decay of manliness.

A still larger mental effect of the Revolutionary War was the high place of political and social influence accorded, for many years after its successful conclusion, to military men who had taken part in it. Throughout history, this has been one of the stock results of warfare. All will remember our twelve soldier-presidents, and the older among us will remember how, for thirty years after the Civil War, there was no qualification for civil office, or at any rate, no qualification for candidacy, more valuable than a military title derived from that conflict. So it was with the Revolutionary War, and even more so, for, it should be remembered, to the minds of that time our national history began with the Revolution. When one went back beyond the year 1775, he lost himself in the confusion of thirteen separate streams. Therefore the men who had made the Revolutionary War successful were like the eponymous heroes who had founded Grecian cities. They had begun the history of a nation, and were entitled to an exceptional share of military glory.

The circumstances of warfare in those days, it should also be remembered, were such as lent themselves readily to the acquirement of military glory. The weapons were of short range. Battles were fought by daylight. The numbers engaged were so moderate, the field of each battle was so little extended, that the display of individual valor could be frequent and conspicuous. In such respects, the character of military struggles changed little from the time of Hector and Agamemnon till the latter years of the nineteenth century. When Horatius smote down Astur, when Ney led in person the last charge of the Guards at Waterloo, or when Armistead and Garnett at Gettysburg fell at the head of their brigades, whole armies saw and remembered. Throughout all these years military glory was within the grasp of every officer. Now, when armies in trenches and dugouts, or in the darkness of midnight, contend against invisible enemies miles away in front, and the proper post of a general officer is at the telephone instrument, miles in the rear, the opportunity to acquire personal fame in warfare has almost disappeared. The officer who passionately desires the limelight cannot obtain it by visible exploits against the enemy in the open field, but only by attacking his superiors in the front pages of the newspapers.

It would seem too large a digression if one were to discuss at length the effects of this disappearance or almost entire reduction of the soldier's opportunity for individual fame, but in passing one may draw attention to the powerful aid it brings to the cause of the world's peace. No one can review in his mind the warlike literature of previous ages, the rhetoric of military proclamations, the animating spirit of war songs and war poems, without perceiving how strong an incitement to warfare has come from the desire and hope of military glory. Under present conditions, that whole motive has practically disappeared from the world, to the world's great benefit. Of the many noble youths who eight years ago went over to the fields of France, hardly any, I think we should all agree, were influenced by that traditional motive. Did anyone ever hear any of them use the words "glory" or "laurels" or "renown"? They went to war as to an imperative but regrettable duty that must be conscientiously performed, and the scene they saw before them was not a brilliant garden of laurels but an unattractive and prosaic sea of mud.

A hundred and fifty years ago, however, military distinction was an attractive and potent reality. Those who had attained it in the Revolutionary War received from their fellow-citizens honors and offices and influence that often were well deserved and well exercised, but in not a few cases extended much beyond the qualifications for high position or beyond the time when it could suitably be retained.

Other influences from the war sprang from the fact that it was waged with the aid of French allies. Gratitude for French aid made beloved friends of those who fifteen years before had been the enemies of all English America. French officers, usually pleased with America, charmed both American men and American women. French fashions became the vogue, and French manners had their influence. French books, especially those of Voltaire and Raynal, were sold in all the bookshops. French newspapers began a precarious existence. French army surgeons taught the medical fraternity in America much that was useful. The American Philosophical Society admitted many Frenchmen as members, and the American Academy of Arts and Sciences was founded at Boston on the model of institutions of similar purpose in France. The need of learning the French language was widely felt. Twenty-six teachers of French in the United States in 1785 are known. The College of William and Mary established a chair of that language, the first in the United States, in 1779. Harvard College the next year gave it the status of a regular though elective subject of instruction, and in 1782 arranged that freshmen and sophomores might take it instead of Hebrew.

What influence upon education in general the Revolution exercised it would be difficult to say, so various were the conditions, so little systematic the organization. The Duke of La Rochefoucauld notes already in 1794 the habit of speaking of the United States as "the most enlightened nation of the world," and he notes it with tolerance, admitting a large degree of popular intelligence. Whatever foundation the boast may have had was probably due more largely to the rapid increase of newspapers and other printing which was mentioned in the last lecture, conjoined with the quickness of mind naturally produced by pioneer life and race-mixture, than to any improvements which the period of warfare can have brought to the colonial systems of elementary or secondary education. Inevitably many schools and academies must have been broken up, and though we see evidences of much desire for educational progress, it would need much time for fruition.

In respect to college education, we can see our way somewhat more clearly. When the war opened there were in the colonies nine colleges—Harvard, the College of William and Mary, Yale, the College of New Jersey (Princeton), King's College (Columbia), the College of Philadelphia (now the University of Pennsylvania), Rhode Island College (now

Brown University), Dartmouth and Queen's College (Rutgers). During the war there was no addition to this list, and indeed some of these suspended operations. But within eight years from the fall of Yorktown, the number of colleges in the country was nearly doubled, by the addition of eight new ones, chiefly founded by those religious denominations which had been actively engaged in the work of perfecting their internal organization. Of the eight, one was planted in Pennsylvania, Dickinson College, then Presbyterian; four in Maryland, Washington College at Chestertown, St. John's College at Annapolis, the Catholic college at Georgetown, and a Methodist college at Abington, burned down a few years later and never rebuilt; two in Virginia, Washington and Hampden-Sidney; and one at Charleston, South Carolina. In the next decade half-a-dozen more were founded, and, as the century turned, the ambitious American mind, full of pride and hope, began to label its infant institutions with the name of universities.

Before discussing the effects of the American Revolution upon religion, it will be useful to glance for a moment at the state and relations of the various religious bodies in the colonies at the time when the war broke out. Unamerican as the idea of religious establishment seems in our day, in nine of the colonies there was in 1770 an established church. But this meant different things in different colonies. In New Hampshire, Massachusetts and Connecticut it was the Congregational Church that was established by law and supported by general taxation, and the majority of the people belonged to it, though there were considerable numbers of Baptists, and many Episcopalians in Connecticut,

Boston, and Portsmouth. Of the six colonies in which the English Church was established, there was none in which its adherents constituted a majority of the people. In Virginia it included perhaps half, the Presbyterians, Baptists, Methodists, and Moravians another half. In Maryland the dissenters were more numerous than the churchmen; in New York, New Jersey, the Carolinas, and Georgia much more numerous. In New York the English Church was established in only a few localities outside of the city, and in New Jersey it cannot properly be said to have been established at all. In all the southern colonies the whole body of the people were called upon to pay taxes for the support of the ministers of the established church, though it was the church of a minority. This was a great grievance, and was bitterly resented.

It is quite true that in the colonies south of Virginia the laws regarding tithes were not strictly regarded, and that in all colonies a practical toleration had been secured, after a long struggle. Yet much remained to make the situation of a dissenter highly uncomfortable. Take North Carolina for example. The witty Colonel Byrd said that it had "a climate where no clergyman can breathe, any more than spiders in Ireland." At the end of the colonial period, there were but six Episcopal clergymen in the province. The Presbyterians and the Moravians each were as numerous as the Anglicans, and the Quakers more so. Yet all were by law obliged to contribute to the support of the English clergymen. Governor Tryon had surely no intention of being humorous when he said to the assembly, "I profess myself a warm advocate for toleration, but I never heard of toleration in any country made use of as an argument to exempt Dissenters from bearing their share of the support of the established religion." Until 1766 it is actually true that no marriages were legal that were not solemnized by the Episcopal clergymen, and even then the privilege was extended only to the Presbyterians, and on condition that the fees went to the Anglicans. Another law forbade any man to teach school unless he were an Episcopalian, though the province was in the most abject need of education.

In Pennsylvania and in Rhode Island entire religious freedom prevailed. In the former, Quakers, Lutherans, Presbyterians, Episcopalians, Baptists, Moravians, Dunkards, Mennonites, and Catholics lived side by side without difficulty. In Rhode Island the Baptists were the leading denomination, but Quakers, Episcopalians, and Congregationalists flourished undisturbed. Taking the thirteen colonies together, the most careful enumeration (the results of which have not yet been published) gives a total of 3105 religious organizations, about a thousand each in New England, the Middle Colonies, and the South. Of these, 658 congregations were of the Congregationalist order, nearly all in New England, 543 were Presbyterian, 498 Baptist, 480 Anglican, 295 of the Society of Friends, 261 German and Dutch Reformed, 151 Lutheran, and 50 Catholic.

With all this varied mixture of religions, the shock of revolution would necessarily loosen the bonds which bound unwilling multitudes to any church establishment with which they had no sympathy. In New England the established church was not immediately threatened, for it was the church of the majority, and most of its clergy and adherents were on the American side, while its opponents were also the opponents of the Revolution. Accordingly in New Hampshire the Congregational Church continued to be established until 1817, in Connecticut till 1818, in Massachusetts even down to 1833. In the colonies where the church established by law was the Episcopal Church, disestablishment was effected with comparative ease, except in Virginia. Here the established church had perhaps as many communicants as dissenters, and it had the warm support of many influential men, some of whom doubtless felt, as did one whose opinion has been quoted and thus preserved to us: "Sure I am, that no *gentleman* will choose to go to Heaven otherwise than by the way of the established church."

Disestablishment in Virginia was a natural consequence of the doctrine laid down in the Virginia Declaration of Rights of 1776, but some difficulty was to be expected in immediately carrying out that doctrine. George Mason's original draft of that Declaration had pronounced for a complete toleration. A very young member named James Madison, who had been much impressed by the wrongs of the dissenters in concrete cases which he had known, urged something more than mere toleration, and the Declaration as finally passed read as follows. "16. That religion, or the duty which we owe to our Creator, and the manner of discharging it, can be directed only by reason and conviction, not by force or violence, and therefore all men are equally entitled to the free exercise of religion, according to the dictates of conscience, and that it is the mutual duty of all to practise Christian forbearance, love and charity towards each other."

It was asked in convention whether this was meant as a prelude to an attack on the established church, and Patrick

Henry declared that it was not. Nevertheless such principles led inevitably to the equality of all religious bodies before the law, and the peculiar privileges of the established church were sure to be soon assailed. This was the more likely to happen because so many of the Episcopal clergy were Tories. Moreover, their own character was in many cases to blame for the feeling against them. Very likely the stories regarding the roystering and fox-hunting Virginia parsons of the eighteenth century are exaggerated. Probably we must not regard as typical the one who, after dinner every Sunday with the chief planter of his neighborhood, was tied in his chaise and sent home with a servant, nor that other and most humorous man of God who, after thrashing his vestry soundly, added insult to injury by preaching to them next day from the text, "And I contended with them, and cursed them, and smote certain of them, and plucked off their hair." But there is enough evidence to show that there was much looseness among the Virginian clergy, and, if not much evil living, at any rate much want of zeal. Otherwise it would be impossible to explain the rapid progress of dissent. At the beginning of the century dissenters had had no places of worship in the colony except three or four Presbyterian meeting-houses and one of the Quakers, and now half the population were dissenters. The Presbyterians were the first to become numerous and active, especially as the upland portions of the country became filled with a population of Irish or Scotch-Irish immigrants. Soon the Moravians, Baptists, and New Lights began to multiply, and Germans, Lutheran or Reformed, from Pennsylvania. The vitality of these sects was greater than that of the established church, and they rapidly gathered strength for the coming conflict, in which, too, they were sure to be aided by many Episcopal laymen whose political principles of hostility to all privileges influenced them more strongly than regard for the special interests of their church.

In the conflict that now arose, feelings of the most extreme warmth were engaged. The dissenters had received hard measure at the hands of governors and legislatures which for a long time had been almost without exception composed of Episcopalians. Actual persecutions even had been visited upon them, such as one may see recorded in the quaint and engaging narrative of Robert Semple. Marriages by their clergy were invalid. They were taxed for the support of a church concerning which it was but natural for them to feel that its services to the cause of Christianity were much less considerable than their own more enthusiastic labors. Accordingly they were eager to pull down the establishment altogether: "There had been a time," says Semple, "when they would have been satisfied, to have paid their tithes, if they could have had liberty of conscience; but now, the crisis was such, that nothing less than a total overthrow of all ecclesiastical distinctions, would satisfy their sanguine hopes. Having started the decaying edifice, every dissenter put to his shoulder, to push it into irretrievable ruin." They were sure of the most ardent support of Jefferson and of Madison.

Scarcely had the first legislature under independence begun its sessions, when petitions for religious freedom began to pour in upon it. Among them is one petition which was said to be signed by ten thousand freemen. Several thousand names still remain attached to it, and the signatures, examined with care, or indeed the very number of such signatures to this and other similar petitions, show that the dissenters were by no means an illiterate portion of the population. On the other hand there is a petition to the contrary from a considerable number of the clergy of the established church, and a Methodist petition upon the same side, signed by one of their ministers in behalf of nearly three thousand Methodists. The clergymen represent that the public faith had been virtually pledged to them for the receiving of due recompense for their services as long as they lived, that they had entered into holy orders upon that understanding and were now practically incapacitated for any other calling, and argue strongly in favor of an establishment upon grounds of public utility.

Upon the other side the ablest memorial presented was that of the chief organization of the Virginian Presbyterians, the celebrated Hanover Presbytery. Baptists and Quakers and Mennonites joined with them. The struggle which followed was afterward characterized by Jefferson, who had surely seen many political struggles, as the severest he had ever witnessed. The issue of it was the passage of an act by which dissenters were exempted from taxes for the support of the established church. It was made lawful for ministers of other churches to celebrate the rite of marriage. All acts for providing the salaries of the clergy were suspended. It was thought that, as a possible solution of the matter, a general tax might be levied for the support of religion, but each taxpayer be left free to declare to which religious body his taxes should be turned over. Patrick Henry favored this, and so, I believe, did General Washington. But the plan was postponed till after the Revolution, and then failed. Instead, Mr. Jefferson succeeded in securing the passage of his act for establishing religious freedom, of which he was so proud that he ordered the inscription on his grave-stone to read: "Thomas Jefferson, Author of the Declaration of American Independence, of the Statute of Virginia for Religious Freedom, and Father of the University of Virginia." This statute, after a highly rhetorical preamble, characteristic of Mr. Jefferson, provides that "no man shall be compelled to frequent or support any religious worship, place, or ministry whatsoever; nor shall be enforced, restrained, molested, or burdened in his body or goods, nor shall otherwise suffer on account of his religious opinions or belief; but that all men shall be free to profess, and by argument to maintain, their opinions in matters of religion."

In Maryland, in New York, and in the southernmost colonies the Anglican Church was disestablished early in the Revolutionary contest, and with comparatively little difficulty. Everywhere it involved a large measure of hardship to certain individuals, but surely no one can be sorry that the system of voluntary support took the place of legal compulsion, especially of legal compulsion to support an unacceptable church. If religious freedom and equality is America's chief contribution to the world's civilization, as has been conspicuously declared—and surely much could be said for this view—great honor belongs to the men of the Revolutionary period, for then it was, more than at any other time, that this principle, so distinctive of America and so invaluable to her prosperity and development, was put into actual practice.

It would be absurd to affirm, however, that religious freedom and equality had yet reached their full development in America. In three of the four New England states, the Congregational churches continued to be established. In Massachusetts and Maryland no man could take any office without subscribing a declaration that he believed in the Christian religion. In Pennsylvania he must also declare (and this applied to all members of the legislature also) that he believed the Scriptures to be given by divine inspiration. Delaware required a Trinitarian test for both officers and legislators. In New Jersey, North Carolina, and South Carolina, they must be Protestants. "No person," says the constitution of North Carolina, "who shall deny the being of God, or the truth of the Protestant religion, or the divine authority either of the Old or New Testaments, or who shall hold religious principles incompatible with the freedom or safety of the State, shall be capable of holding any office or place of trust or profit in the civil department within this State." Yet in most cases these restrictions disappeared before many years, and substantially the battle of religious liberty was won.

So far we have been speaking of positive gains which came to American religion by means of the Revolution. It is not to be supposed that there were not also losses. Many writers agree in declaring that service in the patriotic army was naturally demoralizing. Outside the army, too, attention was turned away from religious things. Congregations were broken up. In many cases their ministers went to the war as chaplains, or fled to the enemy as Tories. Sometimes they entered on more belligerent service. Two of the Episcopal clergymen of Virginia became colonels in the Revolutionary army, and one of them became a brigadier-general.

Many churches were destroyed, injured, or desecrated during the war. The Old South Church in Boston was used as a riding-school by the British cavalry. So was one of the Dutch Reformed churches in New York City, while another was used as a hospital. Presbyterian churches suffered especially, for the Presbyterians were almost all Whigs. Indeed, it is said that if the British soldiers discovered a large Bible and a metrical version of the psalms of David in any house, they took it as prima facie evidence that it was the home of a rebel. The Presbyterian church at Newtown, Long Island, had its steeple sawed off, and was used as a prison and guardhouse till it was torn down and its boards used for the construction of soldiers' huts. That at Crumpond was burned to save it from being occupied by the enemy. That of Mount Holly was burned. That of Princeton was seized by the Hessians, and stripped of its pews and gallery for fuel. A fireplace was built in it, and a chimney carried up through the roof. Washington, supposing that it would be defended against him, planted his cannon near it and began firing into it. The church at Babylon, Long Island, was torn down by the enemy for military purposes. That of Elizabeth was burned. The Presbyterian churches in New York City were made into prisons, or used by the British officers for stabling their horses. More than fifty places of worship in various parts of the country were entirely destroyed by the enemy during the course of the war. Even where the church-edifice was unharmed, the congregation was often scattered. Thus, at Albany, which suffered little from the war, Presbyterian services almost altogether ceased, and with the return of peace the church had to be organized anew. On the other hand Episcopal churches were likely to suffer because of the Toryism of their pastors or people.

Even if no harm were intentionally done, it was likely that, in a country having but few large public buildings of any other kind, churches would be pressed into service as hospitals, barracks, and storehouses, and thus exposed to destruction in greater measure than usual. Our heroic ancestors, it will be remembered, scorned the effeminacy of warming their churches, so that the chance of their burning down was not great. Military uses increased this chance immediately.

In Maryland and Virginia war and disestablishment operated together to disorganize the Anglican Church. When the Revolution broke out, there were in Maryland forty-four parishes and forty-four incumbents. When it closed, but eighteen or twenty rectors remained. In Virginia there had been ninety-five parishes, one hundred and four churches and chapels, and ninety-one clergymen of the established church. When the contest was over, a large number of the churches were found to be destroyed or injured beyond repairing. The reader of good Bishop Meade's interesting old book on the old churches, ministers, and families of Virginia will remember how often he laments the continued disuse and disrepair of churches which fell into dilapidation at the time of the Revolution. Of the ninety-five parishes, twenty-three were extinct or forsaken when the war ended, and thirty-four more were without ministerial services. Of the ninety-one clergymen only twenty-eight remained who had weathered the storm, and of these, only fifteen continued in the same churches which they had occupied before the Revolution. Thirteen had been driven by violence or want from their old parishes but had found a refuge in some other parish which happened to be vacant and was perhaps less reduced by the war. For many years after the war, the church was at a low ebb in Virginia. Bishop Meade tells us that when he was ordained at Williamsburg, one Sunday in winter, as the Bishop and he were making their way to the old church, they met a number of the students of William and Mary College with guns on their shoulders and dogs at their sides going out hunting, while at the same time one of the citizens was filling his ice-house. The windows of the church were broken, and the congregation consisted of two ladies and about fifteen gentlemen. In Richmond, for several years after the war, the church was seldom used, and the only religious services held, in a population amounting to three or four thousand, were Episcopal and Presbyterian services held on alternate Sundays in a room in the state capitol.

Nor was this deadness confined to the Episcopal Church, in which case it might possibly be attributed to the losses which that church had suffered through disestablishment. Travellers as various as the royalist French Duke of La Rochefoucauld, the republican Brissot de Warville, the English manufacturer Henry Wansey all unite in testifying to it as common among the Congregationalists and Presbyterians as well, in Boston, in New York, and in Philadelphia. The old historian of the Virginia Baptists tells us, in quaint phrases, that "the war, though very propitious to the liberty of the Baptists, had an opposite effect upon the life of religion among them. From whatever cause," he says, "certain it is, that they suffered a very wintry season. With some few exceptions, the declension was general throughout the state. The love of many waxed cold. Some of the watchmen fell, others stumbled, and many slumbered at their posts. Iniquity greatly abounded." There is much to support what the famous Marquis of Pescara said to the papal legate, "It is impossible for men to serve Mars and Christ at the same time." It is possible for individuals, but it is difficult for a whole generation.

However great the apathy which had fallen upon the spirit of American religion, it would surely recover, as the nation itself gradually recovered from the ravages and injuries of war. A nation inspired by the sense of a career of future greatness can seldom fail to develop active religious life in some form, and it was certain that America would sometime become religious, even if it were not so in the years immediately after the Revolution. Meanwhile it was possible for it to be developing its ecclesiastical systems, and indeed natural for it to do so. The whole period from the close of the war to the year 1789 was, it is familiar, a period of constitution-making in the United States. It is perhaps less familiar that this period of activity in the making of constitutions for civil government was also marked by great activity in the framing of constitutions for ecclesiastical government. The complete separation of church and state in America, and our division into numerous denominations, should not blind us to the fact that there is after all a certain unity in American church history, as well as a frequent connection between it and the civil history of the nation. Whether this can be made out at other times or not, it certainly can be seen at the particular period we are considering. The great fact of national independence forced several churches to recast their forms of government, and the occupation of men's minds with problems of national organization could not fail to stir them up to improvements in their religious organization, in a country where, as in America, the clergy were far from being a class apart, uninfluenced by what was going on around them and totally separate from the laity.

Let us begin with the Episcopal Church. If it had really needed a bishop before the war—and about this there had been an agitation that alarmed many members of other churches—how much more now! It was not possible that the independent United States of America should continue to be a part of the diocese of the bishop of London. It was not possible that the ministers of that church should go on reading the prayers for King George and the other parts of the service which assumed a monarchical government. So began the movement for an American episcopate. That political grounds had had the chief part in the previous opposition to this movement, is shown by the fact that there was no opposition now. But how to secure the ordination of bishops was a question of much difficulty. Indeed it now seemed impossible to obtain from England the ordination of priests even. Dr. Franklin, with his curious inability to perceive religious distinctions, made an amusing attempt, through the papal nuncio in Paris, to see if a young correspondent of his could not be ordained in the Catholic Church without becoming a member of its communion. Adams made a more promising attempt to obtain for such young men an ordination through the Danish bishops. The King of Denmark was found willing. But meantime the movement for an American episcopate came rapidly forward. Bishop Seabury was consecrated by the non-juring Scottish bishops. A meeting of the clergy at New York in 1784 began the framing of a constitution for the Protestant Episcopal Church in America. Just as in the case of the Constitution of the United States, inter-state jealousies hindered union. But, by a somewhat similar process, conventions held at Philadelphia in 1785, 1786, and 1789 adjusted all differences, and united in a federal union the various dioceses, as the various states were being united in the more famous federal union of the United States. In the maintenance of the state system, in the relations of the two houses in the General Convention, and in many minor details, the constitution adopted for the church showed the influence of the Constitution just adopted for the civil government of the country.

Another church which was obliged to place itself upon a new basis was the Catholic Church. Hitherto the Catholic clergy in America had been under the control of the vicar apostolic of London. But when Great Britain had acknowledged the independence of the United States, the new vicar apostolic of London disclaimed all jurisdiction over them, and candidates for orders found themselves in the same predicament as the young Episcopalians. The Catholic clergy met in Maryland in 1783 and discussed plans of organization. In France there was some talk of their being annexed to a French vicariate apostolic. But more judicious counsels prevailed at Rome, and in 1784 the Catholic Church in the United States was by decree of the Congregation of the Propaganda erected into a distinct body, with Father John Carroll, cousin of Charles Carroll of Carrollton, as prefect apostolic. Later, in 1790, he was made bishop of Baltimore, and the new organization of the Catholic Church in America was complete.

So entirely had the Methodist body in America been under the control of John Wesley that, among them also, the fact of American independence made necessary a radical change of organization. In 1773, when the first American Methodist conference was held, the society had ten circuits and sixteen hundred members. In 1783, in spite of the prevailing apathy in other religious bodies, they were five times as numerous, and it became difficult to keep them to certain of Wesley's rules. Wesley always wished his followers to remain in the Church of England, but the American Methodists often found it impossible to receive the communion or to obtain the baptism of their children if they must depend on the Episcopal clergymen. Wesley, therefore, after much hesitation, consecrated Thomas Coke as superintendent of the American Methodists, with powers of ordination, and assigned the same position to Francis Asbury. At the famous Christmas Conference held at Baltimore in 1784 Asbury was ordained, and an independent organization set in operation for the Methodist Church in the United States. Presently the title of "bishop" superseded that of "superintendent." The society dropped from its minutes that curious clause, which paints to the life the spirit of the earliest Methodism: "During the life of the Rev. Mr. Wesley, we acknowledge ourselves his sons in the gospel, ready, in matters belonging to church government, to obey his commands." The general conferences gradually gave more and more settled shape to the internal regulations of the society, till finally it had perfected its organization as an independent American church.

Other religious bodies felt less pressure than these from the mere fact of independence to give themselves new form. But the constitution-making spirit was in the air, and hardly any escaped it. One denomination after another took on a more comprehensive or more highly developed organization. The main body of the Presbyterians in 1788 provided for this completer development, and in 1789 the first General Assembly of the Presbyterian Church in the United States convened at Philadelphia. The Dutch Reformed Church, which had obtained its independence of Europe before the Revolution began, held its first General Synod in 1792. Even the seceding Presbyterians of the strict Covenanting school attempted in 1782 to unite, though, unhappily yet characteristically, the attempt only resulted in the production of three bodies in the place of two. The Freewill Baptists set up a yearly meeting in 1792. The Universalists held their first general convention in 1786. The United Brethren in Christ held their first formal conference at Baltimore in 1789. Even the Baptists, whose plan of independent congregations lent itself ill to superior organization, instituted in Virginia, in 1784, a General Committee to act for the whole in certain matters. In short, there was no important religious body, except the Congregationalists, which did not, in just these years, go through something of this process. Evidently there was no escaping the general impulse which in those years was leading the Americans, in all possible ways, to draw together in better forms of organization.

In the election sermon already alluded to, preached by President Stiles before the General Assembly of Connecticut in 1783, the preacher makes plain his expectation that the future of religion in the United States will belong, not far from equally, to the three denominations of the Congregationalists, the Presbyterians, and the Episcopalians. Great would be his astonishment could he see the numerical proportions in our day, the first, second, and third places occupied by the Catholics, Methodists, and Baptists, of whom he made little account, the denominations which ranked foremost in his prophecy now standing eighth, fourth, and seventh. He could not foresee the workings of democracy and immigration, and failed to imagine that the future in such a country would fall, not to denominations whose traditions required an educated and therefore expensive ministry, but to those whose system could be flexibly adapted to the conditions of frontier settlement.

It is not intended in these lectures, nor is the lecturer competent, to discuss at length the influence of the Revolution upon theological thought in the United States. But I will, in mere passing mention, call attention to the fact that, of the religious bodies which in this period were growing in numbers and zeal, four (that is to say, all but one) were anti-Calvinistic—namely, the Methodists, the Universalists, the Unitarians, and the Freewill Baptists. This is not without significance. In a period when the special privileges of individuals were being called in question or destroyed, there would naturally be less favor for that form of theology which was dominated by the doctrine of the especial election of a part of mankind, a growing favor for those forms which seemed more distinctly to be based upon the idea of the natural equality of all men. But I dwell upon the thought no farther than to bring it forward as one more illustration of that general thesis which in fact underlies this whole series of lectures—the thesis that all the varied activities of men in the same country and period have intimate relations with each other, and that one cannot obtain a satisfactory view of any one of them by considering it apart from the others.

INDEX

Adams, John, 12, 66, 96
Agriculture: in colonies, 27–28,
    50; experimentation in, 48–51;
    societies for promotion of, 51–54
Alfred, King, 48
American Academy of Arts and
    Sciences, 81
American Association, 69
American Philosophical Society, 81
American Revolution: centennial
    observances of, 1; changing
    view of, 2–5; aims of, 6; com-
    pared with French Revolution,
    5–6, 14; trade restrictions as
    cause of, 12; supporters of,
    analyzed, 11–16; age of leaders
    in, 13–14; size of colonial army
    in, 47
—effects of: social, 16–17, 28;
    on slavery, 19–25; economic,
    31–46; on land ownership,
    31–33; on land laws, 36–38;
    on industry, 52–59; on com-
    merce, 62–63, 69–71, 72–73;
    on humanitarianism, 76–77; on
    dueling, 78; on military pres-
    tige, 79; on education, 82–83;
    on religion, 83–100; on theo-
    logical thought, 100
Ames, Fisher, 61
Annapolis Convention (1786), 72
Anti-slavery societies, 22–24
Asbury, Francis, 98

Bank of New York, 64
Bank of North America, 64
Baptists: in trans-Allegheny West,
    43; in colonies, 83, 85, 87;
    opposed to establishment,
    89; postwar decline in church
    attendance, 94; organizational
    changes by, 99
Barlow, Joel, 77
Beccaria, Cesare Bonesana, 77
Belknap, Jeremy, 17
Benezet, Anthony, 21
Brandywine Creek, 60
Brandywine, battle of, 58
Brissot de Warville, Jacques Pierre,
    68, 94
Buffon, Comte de, 51
Burke, Edmund, 7
Byrd, Colonel, 84

Carroll, Charles, of Carrollton, 16,
    97
Carroll, Rev. John, 97
Catholics: in colonies, 85;
    organizational changes by,
    97; numerical proportions
    of, 98
China trade, 68
Christmas Conference (Baltimore,
    1784), 98
Churches: damaged in war, 91–93;
    changes in constitutions and
    organization of, 95–99

[101]

A NOTE ON THE TYPE

THIS BOOK has been composed in Miller, a Scotch Roman typeface designed by Matthew Carter and first released by Font Bureau in 1997. It resembles Monticello, the typeface developed for The Papers of Thomas Jefferson in the 1940s by C. H. Griffith and P. J. Conkwright and reinterpreted in digital form by Carter in 2003.

Pleasant Jefferson ("P. J.") Conkwright (1905–1986) was Typographer at Princeton University Press from 1939 to 1970. He was an acclaimed book designer and AIGA Medalist.

The ornament used throughout this book was designed by Pierre Simon Fournier (1712–1768) and was a favorite of Conkwright's, used in his design of the *Princeton University Library Chronicle*.

GPSR Authorized Representative: Easy Access System Europe - Mustamäe tee
50, 10621 Tallinn, Estonia, gpsr.requests@easproject.com